Dedication

To: *Father Joe Lavin:*
He served both priests
and people.

Since August 16, 1982,
Father Joe intercedes
in eternity for us.

Thanks

To: *My wonderful typists:*
Mom and Dad.
Mrs. Gina Meigs (1998)
Eileen Hering (1999)

TABLE OF CONTENTS

A. INTRODUCTION

B. BACKGROUND OF MATTHEW

Part Six: REJECTION BY JEWS:
 ADMISSION OF GENTILES

Part Seven: THE PASSION

A. INTRODUCTION

CENTRAL PURPOSE

My own prayer centers on the Kingdom, especially the presence and power of Jesus' Kingdom. For many this Kingdom seems so far away. Although people know about the Kingdom, this gift is not a daily experience. They would want the Kingdom as a daily, regular experience, but they aren't able to grasp the gift.

The title: "THE KINGDOM AT HAND" means that the door to the Kingdom is as near as this book. People can't always get to Church. They can't even settle their minds for some prayerful quiet time. At least, they can pick up this book.

Every chapter was written for the busy man or woman who can snatch a few moments for prayer but doesn't have the luxury of a monk.

The reader can begin anywhere, taking in as little or as much as time allows. The book is written to be read by itself or with Matthew's gospel as a companion. The latter is certainly more profitable. Also the reader can be systematic, praying one part each day, or just use the book for random reading. It doesn't matter. The Kingdom is at hand and Jesus wants you to experience His gift. He doesn't set conditions. He takes every chance to open His gift to all.

From that time on Jesus began to proclaim this theme: "Reform your lives! The Kingdom of heaven is at hand." (4:17)

I

THE APPROACH

The chapters of this book are based upon the different sections of Matthew's gospel. Not every verse, nor even every thought, is commented upon. For the sake of style and clarity, seven thoughts from each section were selected.

B. BACKGROUND ON MATTHEW
MATTHEW'S PLAN

He has five major parts in describing Jesus' public ministry. These are preceded by his infancy narrative (Ch 1-2) and followed by his passion account (Ch 26-28). These seven major parts are:

1) Infancy (Ch 1-2)
2) Promulgating the Kingdom (Ch 3-7)
3) Preaching the Kingdom (Ch 8-10)
4) The Mystery of the Kingdom (Ch 11-13:52) (especially its lowliness)
5) The Initial Growth of Believers (Ch 13:53-18)
6) The Division: Rejection by Jews and Admission of Gentiles (Ch 19-25)
7) Passion (Ch 26-28)

FULFILLING THE OLD TESTAMENT

All the New Testament writers were anxious to show Jesus as the fulfillment of the Old Testament. Matthew, however, is the most zealous in this regard. He alludes to or quotes the Old Testament 60 times, believing deeply that every Old Testament text contained some hidden allusion to Jesus. He quotes many Old Testament books, but prefers Isaiah. He also uses the other prophets, the Law and the Psalms widely.

II

HIS THEOLOGY

Matthew's doctrine is clear:

1)   Jesus Christ fulfills the Old Testament
2)   Israel rejects Christ
3)   The Kingdom is given to others
4)   The Church is the new Israel

Matthew's central word is "the Kingdom" which he uses fifty-one times. His using the word "Heaven" (as Kingdom of Heaven) reflects the Jewish substitution of that word for God.

This term "the Kingdom of Heaven" was lost by the early Christians, who substituted words like "Church" or "eternal life." In doing this, a power was lost because the Kingdom could be present, "at hand," and yet future since people "shall enter."

THE CHURCH

By the time Matthew wrote his gospel, the Christian community was already organized. Also, the controversies with Jewish leaders were increasing, causing Matthew to quote the Old Testament so frequently as proof of Jesus' role.

TWO VERSIONS

Scripture scholars hold that two versions of Matthew were written. The first was an Aramaic version containing primarily the sayings of Jesus. Later, after Mark's gospel, the present Greek version of Matthew was written. Matthew's gospel, therefore, contains the original sayings of Jesus, but depends upon Mark's gospel for its order and many narratives.

The gospel has a strong Palestinian character. Many expressions are obviously Semitic. So strong is this Palestinian flavor, that some Church Fathers thought the gospel was written for Jewish converts. This gospel was the favorite of the early Church and used for liturgical service.

CHAPTER 1
THOSE WHO WENT BEFORE (1:1-17)

"A Family record of Jesus Christ, son of David, son of Abraham." (V-1)

Thought

We all have these lists of ancestors that we have never met, but upon whom our existence depends. The same can't be said of Jesus. He was no accident. His existence didn't depend upon a human ancestor. Yet, many were privileged to share in his lineage.

Jesus is real. He is not like the mysterious Melchizedek, king of Salem, who appears and disappears with no mention of ancestors. Jesus is rooted in "a family record."

Application

These writings have one goal - to make Jesus real for you. He is not meant to be a mysterious far-off figure – someone like your ancestors, whom you hardly know. He is Jesus of Nazareth, now risen from the dead. He wants to come to you.

"Abraham was the father of Isaac, Isaac the father of Jacob, Jacob the father of Judah and his brothers." (V-2)

Thought

Many names on the list, you don't know, but these are familiar. Abraham, the father of all Semites; Isaac, the child of the Promise; and Jacob who received the blessing over Esau, because his mother, Rachel, favored him. These were ordinary people who helped change the world because they listened to God.

Application

Everyone should listen to God. Hopefully, through this book, you will learn how to listen. The words you read aren't important. The words you hear inside, the guidance of the Spirit, are vital.

Read these words, but more importantly, pray this book. The written word invites you to listen to God's spoken word within.

"Boaz was the father of Obed, whose mother was Ruth. Obed was the father of Jesse. "(V-5)

Thought
The history of this one verse occupies a whole book of "Ruth." The story is made famous in the song, "Wherever you go." Ruth, the Moabite, makes the difficult decision to return with her mother-in-law, Naomi, to Bethlehem, a culture and a people foreign to her. That decision leads to a marriage with Boaz and a child, Obed, who is the grandfather of David.

Application
God intends a beautiful story for you too. The story, although present in God's mind, is worked out here on earth. The single important factor is true loyalty to the people God has placed in your life. Read the book of Ruth (it has only four chapters), and learn to be loyal. Your own history depends on that.

"David was the father of Solomon, whose mother had been the wife of Uriah." (V-6)

Thought
These names are well-known, but what a difference between these two kings. David knows God and begins with a divided kingdom, gradually bringing the Israelites to a high point of their history.

2

Solomon's heart is turned away from the true God, and the kingdom he received from David is doomed to disunity.

Application

First, you must be brought together before you can bring about unity in your home and your work. Yet you are destined to brokenness and fragmentation without God's power in Jesus. Learn that lesson quickly - only God's power in your life saves you from destruction.

"Josiah became the father of Jechoniah and his brothers at the time of the Babylonian exile." (V-11)

Thought

So much did the Israelites wander from God that in 587 B.C. Jerusalem, that city of strength, fell to its conquerors and the Jewish people were taken into exile. Jeremiah prophesied this. He also told them that they would return, for the conquerors were God's instruments of purification. Everything happened according to this word of the Lord.

Application

God will never give up on you. If you leave Him and walk according to other words, problems will happen. But the problems are another way of God speaking to you, reminding you of your wanderings and calling you back.

"Jacob was the father of Joseph the husband of Mary." (V-16)

Thought

This list began with ordinary people - Abraham, Isaac and Jacob, and ends the same way with the little-known Joseph. Matthew doesn't let him slip into complete anonymity, giving us some stories in these early chapters. Joseph is always there. Ready when needed. Doing the tasks of any husband and father. Really, everyone is on the list because they were a parent.

Application
Don't overlook your parental role. Too many shove this into the background for their career. But what career begets children and when the spotlight goes out on a career, what is left?

Be faithful to your home. To the daily tasks that beget and support life. You never know what your children might become.

"It was of her that Jesus who is called the Messiah was born." (V-16)

Thought
After a stage presentation, the actors and actresses are called out for a bow, beginning with the least and then to the greatest. So Mary completes the list. Jesus kept her hidden during life, but no more. She had the greatest role in the whole story. She believed from the beginning when the angel told her and walked to Calvary to finish the drama.

Application
You have a story with Jesus. First, you have to believe, listening to His word and setting out. Then you have to stay with that word, not letting it slip away from you, but being faithful until the end.

CHAPTER 2
JOSEPH'S DREAM (1:18-24)

"Now this is how the birth of Jesus Christ came about..." (V-18)

Thought

The Father arranged everything for Jesus. He had planned the ancestors. Now He prepared for His birth. During life, the Father took care of Jesus. Even in death, He consoled Him. On the third day, the Father raised Jesus to glory.

Application

All the Father did for Jesus, He will do for you. He arranged your ancestors. He provided for your birth. He will keep you from now until your death. He has a heavenly home for you that is your share in Jesus' Resurrection.

"She was found with child through the power of the Holy Spirit." (V-18)

Thought

The Holy Spirit is God, one with the Father and the Son. He carries out the Father's decrees. He brings about the Bethlehem mystery. He is ever active, shaping human history by inspiring people to take certain actions. God has not abandoned His creation. He acts directly.

Application

The Spirit inspires you. He molds your thoughts. He brings you the Kingdom. You are not an orphan. You are not left alone to find your way to the Father's house. You are not abandoned in your struggle. The Spirit's power is with you.

"Joseph...decided to divorce her quietly..." (V-19)

Thought

Joseph tried to do everything right. He knew the law but didn't intend to invoke it's harshness. He would act gently and quietly. However, God's plan was beyond Joseph's ideas.

Application

You have certain thoughts and plans. Bring them to God. He will take you beyond your original dream. He will show you a better way. Don't limit God by your own plans when He would have you act quite differently.

"...Suddenly the angel of the Lord appeared in a dream..." (V-20)

Thought

Inspired dreams happen frequently in Scripture. Why is that? Why do people have to be dreaming to experience God? While asleep, people can't cling to their own thoughts. The mind is free, able to be drawn to the Creator.

Application

God always draws your thoughts to Himself. He wants you to raise your heart and mind to Him. Don't cling to your thoughts. Don't fill your mind with only worldly concerns. Seek the Kingdom. Turn your thoughts to God.

"...It is by the Holy Spirit that she has conceived this child." (V-10)

Thought

Already, Scripture has twice mentioned the Holy Spirit. The Father's plan for Jesus is just unfolding. The Spirit is center stage. He has brought about the mystery which brings salvation to the whole world.

Application
You received this Spirit at Baptism; again at Confirmation. He is the first results of the Eucharist. He is Jesus' gift, your share in the Kingdom. He abides, remains, inspires, changes you and is your new life.

"...They shall call him Emmanuel" a name which means "God is with us" (V-23)

Thought
This chapter's message isn't left in doubt. The name is translated "God is with us", says this chapter. This is what every Scriptural chapter says. He is with us without end. He abides, is close, never goes AWAY.

Application
God is with you, in your home, your work, your fears and your hopes. He is with you in health and in illness. You can't escape Him. You can't go any place where He isn't. Scripture says clearly what already is: "God is with you."

"When Joseph awoke, he did as the angel of the Lord had directed him..." (V-24)

Thought
God's work began in a dream. The completion required that Joseph awake and become a free instrument. The dream revealed God's will. Joseph had to regain his freedom to do that will. The dream was the beginning, completed only by Joseph's fidelity.

Application

Don't let God's works be incomplete in you. Don't let God's stirrings in you bear no results.

Be open to His words. Listen. Ponder. Seek to know your part. Cooperate fully so God's beginning gift is complete.

CHAPTER 3
THE MAGI'S SEARCH (2:1-12)

"... Astrologers...arrived...inquiring, `Where is the newborn King of the Jews?" (V-1-2)

Thought

Questions abound. People ask themselves, "What am I to eat" and "What am I to wear?" They also want to know what they should do with their life. These are nature's questions. The astrologers are asking the Kingdom's question, "Where is the newborn King of the Jews?"

Application

If you are alive to the Kingdom, you should have some questions. "How can I find Jesus?" "Where should I serve Him?" "Is He satisfied with me?" "Am I doing His will?" These are the searching questions. When these are present, you are seeking the Kingdom.

"At this news King Herod became greatly disturbed..." (V-3)

Thought

His disturbance was from the Kingdom. He feared. His selfish lifestyle was threatened. His world was shaken by a new born child. Panic set in. His peace gave way to anxiety.

Application

Events can disrupt your life, yet their power isn't absolute. You shouldn't be totally under their sway. Build your life upon Jesus' Kingdom. Choose now what doesn't pass away. The future events won't entirely dominate you.

"...Go and get detailed information about the Child..." (V-8)

Thought

God wants to be found. He gladly reveals Himself. He gives clues, hints, directions - whatever is needed. Herod wants this "detailed information" for selfish reasons. God won't reveal anything to him. He will hide the Child.

Application

Seek God with purity of heart. Jesus will gladly show you how to find Him. He will open to you the Kingdom. Put aside this day whatever is self-seeking. Set out on your search to glorify God. The Kingdom will be revealed to you.

"They were overjoyed at seeing the star." (V-10)

Thought

Joy is the Spirit's gift, the result of finding God. The world has a joy, but it's a feeling derived from gaining money, power or fame. These will pass away and bring with them anxieties.

Application

What brings you joy? Examine what you rejoice in. Is your joy from the world or from the Kingdom? Do you know the Kingdom's joys? Do you know the feeling of finding God, of experiencing His care, of doing His

*will. Until you experience the Kingdom's joys, you will
never seek and never find.*

"...and on entering the house, found the child with Mary, his Mother." (V-11)

Thought
God doesn't play "hide and seek." He doesn't demand a
long search before people find Him. He is not the God
of absence. He has drawn near to everyone in the
Bethlehem gift.

Application
*Stop wasting time on useless goals. You were made for
Jesus. Your first task is to come to Him. He isn't far
from you. Just begin to search and you will find Him.
Then your real life begins.*

"Then they opened their coffers and presented Him with gifts." (V-11)

Thought
From the beginning of their call to the conclusion of
their task, these wise men responded completely to
God. They believe. They set out in faith. They lose
their way but persevere. When they find Jesus, they
open their coffers.

Others have never believed or set out. Others didn't
persevere. Some find Jesus, but aren't willing to pay
the price of discipleship.

Application
*Don't hold on to your possessions. When you find
Jesus give Him everything. Empty yourself out. Give
away what you have. Only your empty coffer can fully
receive.*

"They received a message in a dream not to return to Herod." (V-12)

Thought

After receiving Jesus' gifts, the person must protect that treasure. the person cannot expose these riches to temptation. The person should guard them by listening to God.

Jesus asks people to seek, so they can acquire some spiritual discernment. Without that wisdom, the newly-acquired riches will be lost.

Application

What gifts have you received? Do you protect them? God led you to those gifts. Do you allow God to lead you to their protection?

Seeking and finding Jesus are the beginning. Remaining with Him and protecting His gifts are your daily task.

You who have listened to God to find Him, listen to Him now so you don't lose His presence.

11

CHAPTER 4
TRAGEDY AND RESPONSE (2:13-23)

"Get up, take the child and his mother, and flee to Egypt." (V-13)

Thought
God's actions upon us are always loving, but not always gentle. An urgency exists. The child is endangered. Nothing is preferred above the child's safety and all is sacrificed to preserve that safety.

Application
God has a single-mindedness toward you. He wants you with Himself forever and ever in His kingdom. No matter what it takes, He will do anything to get you there. Sometimes, that "anything" involves jolting you, in the middle of the night, or whenever necessary.

"Joseph got up and took the child and his mother and left that night for Egypt." (V-14)

Thought
We don't give Joseph enough credit. Everything seems so simple - an angel comes, gives a message and off they go. We gloss over the human questions - How did Joseph hear God's word? When was he supposed to act? How will he fulfill the directions?

Application
Every day God guides you. You don't have angels giving you commands, but within you are God's promptings, inspirations and enlightenments. Still human questions exist. When? How? Where? Be open to God's promptings. Take the questions one by one. Sometimes the prompting is for now. Sometimes they are promptings for the future.

"He ordered the massacre of all the boys two years old and under in Bethlehem and its environs." (V-16)

Thought

Through the Magi, God entered Herod's life. He was threatened and he responded wrongly. His earthly kingdom was so important that he moved into wide-scale murder.

Application

Every time God speaks to you, in some way He threatens your world. He invites you to exchange your kingdom and your world for His kingdom. Don't respond wrongly. Don't feel threatened by God's word.

"...Rachel bewailing her children; no comfort for her, since they are no more." (V-18)

Thought

What could be worse than children slaughtered cruelly on a massive scale. It makes no sense. Yet, since God placed the power of life and death in our hands, the risk of such tragedies is always present.

Application

There are moments when you suffer, possibly needlessly and cruelly at the hands of another. There is no sense to the suffering, no justification or reason. Also, no "comfort" accompanies the suffering. The only glimmer of light is faith in a Jesus whose own birth occasioned the death of the children and whose own life ended in what seems like a purposeless death.

13

"...Those who had designs on the life of the child are dead." (V-20)

Thought

Everything changes. Even the kings and the powerful pass away. The Lord asks His faithful to be patient, not to take matters into their own hands, but let His hand enter and correct.

Application

There is a time to act and a time to wait. Sometimes it is easier to act than to wait. Be patient and listen to God's will. You are not called to total passivity, but you must seek God's solution to each situation.

"There he settled in a town called Nazareth." (V-23)

Thought

Nazareth (in the north) was not Bethlehem or Jerusalem (in the south), but the time for Jesus to go to Jerusalem would be later. For now, Nazareth was perfect, a quiet place where Jesus could grow among a Jewish population.

Application

God has a design for you. It isn't the plan you would choose. If you let God lead you, He will take you to the perfect place. There you can live in peace, use your talents, and be with those who should be sharing your life.

CHAPTER 5
REFORMING, PREPARING AND BRINGING FORTH FRUIT (3:1-11)

"Reform your lives! The reign of God is at hand." (V-2)

Thought

We resist reform. We like things the way they are, yet God's demands always have a reason. Reform is a preparation for a "reign of God."

Application

Certain things have to change in your life. Some adjustments must be made. You can focus on the first part of the verse and grow discouraged, or you can keep your eyes on "the reign of God." That's the goal.

"A herald's voice in the desert: `Prepare the way of the Lord, make straight his paths.'" (V-3)

Thought

Where is the desert today? Where is the voice of John the Baptizer? The desert is in the loneliness, the anxiety, the insecurity, the fears, the searching. The voice is in the teaching of the Church, and the prompting of the Holy Spirit within.

Application

When you experience your personal desert, don't grow discouraged. Listen for the voice. If you can't hear God's voice by yourself, seek out a priest, a believing friend or a word of Scripture. God cannot always save you from desert moments, but God can always speak to you in those moments.

"At that time Jerusalem, all Judea, and the whole region around the Jordan were going out to him." (V-5)

Thought

John's voice could only be heard by those nearby. How limited! Those who came from a distance would naturally be fewer in number. Today that word has gone forth to all the earth, for all to hear.

Application

You possibly have never been to Jerusalem or the Jordan, yet you know John's words. Listen to them today! They are special words that will open to you the Kingdom.

"They were being baptized by him in the Jordan River as they confessed their sins. "(V-6)

Thought

At the preaching of John, they repented. John, however, had only a message of repentance. No Messiah yet! No full gift of the Holy Spirit yet! Just a Baptism of repentance. Soon, John will pass off the scene.

Application

Jesus, the Messiah, has come. You have the full message of Good News. How much more should you confess your sins to receive an even greater cleansing?

"...Do not pride yourselves on the claim, `Abraham is our father...'" (V-9)

Thought

The gospels provide many examples of personal reflections. The Pharisees reflected on his good deeds; the publican on his sins; the cleansed leper on how he should give thanks; the rich man on what he had to give up. Here, the Pharisees and Sadducees reflect on their past traditions, using them as an excuse for not responding to John's message.

Application

What do you reflect on? What thoughts and hopes do you consciously call to mind? What do you hold on to? What do you use as an excuse not to hear God's word today?

"...Even now the ax is laid to the root of the tree..." (V-10)

Thought

Everyone loves a tree. It harms no one. It makes no demands. Why would an owner cut it down? Because he could rightly expect some return. He envisions another more fruitful tree in its place.

Application

God is not a hard taskmaster, placing burdens you cannot carry or demanding results you cannot give. He calls you to help Him with His kingdom. He has given you a task, a family to raise or a work to do. If you fulfill that task, He will never uproot you with His ax.

CHAPTER 6
BAPTISM AND BAPTIZER (3:11-17)

"...the one who will follow me is more powerful than I..." (V-11)

Thought

How powerful is Jesus? The Father has given everything into His hands. He is the Lord of all history. He has overcome the power of death itself. At His name, every knee bends and every tongue proclaims Him Lord.

Application

Do you believe in the power of Jesus? Do you want His power in your life? His power is the Kingdom of God in your life. No need to fear any other power. No need to fear any other person. Jesus said to fear only the person who could condemn the soul to everlasting death. If you believe in Jesus' power, you can walk in freedom.

"...he it is who will baptize you in the holy Spirit and fire..." (V-11)

Thought

Jesus comes to do a definite work. He will pour out His Holy Spirit on all mankind. What does this mean? How is human history different because of Pentecost? The Spirit is given, He can't be seen as Jesus was. However, He does His works within those who believe.

Application

The Spirit came at your Baptism, making you a child of God. The Spirit also has definite work. He reminds you that Jesus is LORD. Let Him work within. Be baptized each day in the Spirit that Jesus sent.

"...his winnowing fan is in his hand..." (V-12)

Thought

The winnowing fan throws both the chaff and the good grain into the air. The chaff, because lighter, is blown away. The good grain falls back to the ground. The separation occurs so that the farmer can treat each differently.

Application

You have received the Spirit, who produces only the finest grain. However, other powers at work in you produce chaff. Today, you have a choice. You can live by the Spirit or you can produce chaff that will be blow away and cast into the fire.

"I should be baptized by you, yet you come to me!" (V-14)

Thought

At this point, John was the celebrity. Jesus, still the unknown. Yet, John does not judge by appearances or by the crowds. He sees within and recognizes Jesus as greater than he.

Application

Don't judge by the world's standards, which exalt the powerful, rich and famous. Only God gives true greatness, the Spirit's life within. Also don't be taken up by appearances. The stature of your office, the size of your paycheck or the esteem of others don't make you great. You have one moment of truth, the moment you stand before Jesus. Live this day in His presence.

"...We must do this if we would fulfill all of God's demands." (V-15)

Thought

To Jesus, every command of the Father was important, from the easily accomplished ritual of His Baptism to the heroic accomplishment of the cross. Later, Jesus would tell parables about being faithful in the little things so as to be put in charge of greater.

Application

Today will be filled with little things. You will be tempted to do them poorly or omit them altogether. You can easily set aside the kind word, the call to a friend, the letter to a loved one, the accomplishing of a task. But the little things lead to bigger things. You will only fulfill all God's will if you do these little things.

"This is my beloved Son. My favor rests on him." (V-17)

Thought

Jesus heard these words. They were a human experience, one of the thousand experiences He had here on earth. He held on to these words. He remembered them. He recalled these words in the dark hours of the Passion. He believed them.

Application

Today, you should hear God's voice. It won't thunder from the heavens, but will resound within your heart. Listen. In the quiet, the Father will speak, clear words, consoling words, true words, words you need to know.

CHAPTER 7
DESERT TEMPTATIONS (4:1-11)

Then Jesus was led into the desert by the Spirit to be tempted by the devil. (V-1)

Thought

Jesus quickly lets the Spirit have His way. No holding back. No delays. No just "celebrating Baptism." The Baptism had a purpose. It was the beginning of His mission.

Application

You have received the Spirit. You must be led by Him. Don't delay. Today alone is the right time. Give control of your life over to the Spirit. Yield to His promptings. To claim that you know exactly where you want to go and what you want to do is foolishness. Jesus went where the Spirit led Him.

He fasted forty days and forty nights, and afterward was hungry. (V-2)

Thought

Why did Jesus fast? And for so long? It seems an extreme measure. Because the world is not like the Father originally planned. The original creation didn't contain the struggles we experience today. In times of struggle we all take extreme measures so as not to be overcome.

Application

It would be nice never to be tempted. You would be able to choose God peacefully. Frequently, the struggle can be intense. But Jesus is with you. He has already been in that storm.

"If you are the Son of God, command these stones to turn into bread." (V-3)

Thought
Food, the needed daily sustenance, can become our undoing. Not in the eating, but in what we do to get it. What means people take to insure themselves that they will always have it! Food is the organic symbol of possessiveness, of taking everything to ourselves.

Application
How many things do you cling to? Let trust in God replace your insecurity. He provides for the birds of the air and the lilies of the field. He will provide for you this day. You don't have to take everything into your own hands. You are already in God's hands!

"If you are the Son of God, throw yourself down." (V-6)

Thought
Why do that? Why make a show? Jesus knew that public opinion was not important. The sudden reputation gained from God saving Him would quickly pass. Even His later reputation, built upon years of teaching, healing and miracles would evaporate.

Application
Do you seek too avidly the acclaim of others? Acclaimed today, you will be forgotten tomorrow. Be known by God, other acclaim passes away.

The devil then took him up a very high mountain and displayed before him all the kingdoms of the world in their magnificence. (V-8)

Thought

Every human being fantasizes. He has dreams of what might be. Very few actually have a chance to be known in all the kingdoms of the world. Others find "little kingdoms" that they substitute for God. Everyone, in some way, is tempted to seek his own kingdom.

Application

If you approach this day in simplicity of heart, you won't be fooled by the false kingdoms dangled in front of you. You will see them for what they are. Everything is a poor substitute for God's kingdom in your midst.

At that the devil left him, and angels came and waited on him. (V-11)

Thought

God sends His own comforts. How much we need them. We need money to free us from economic fears; friendship to share our burdens; guidance to show us where to go; rewards to compensate for our struggles.

Application

You should not always be struggling. The time of struggle should give way to victory. Think over your past struggles, the difficult times. Recall the moments you chose to do the right thing. Remember how God blessed you after the struggle was over. You probably didn't realize that angels had come to wait upon you.

CHAPTER 8
THE KINGDOM AND HEALING (4:12-25)

"A people living in darkness will see a great light..." (V-16)

Thought

At last, the Light of the world would begin to overcome the darkness. What had been hidden as a mystery for centuries, and what had been hidden for 30 years since Bethlehem, was about to be revealed. Jesus is the light for everyone born into this world.

Application

Without Jesus, you walk in darkness. No longer do you have to walk that way. Ask Jesus to come into your life. Don't curse the darkness. Overcome it by the gift the Father has given you.

"Reform our lives? The kingdom of heaven is at hand." (V-17)

Thought

Reforming our lives is a response to the gift at hand. How much we reform depends on how clearly we see that the Kingdom is at hand; that the Bridegroom is coming; that Jesus is already in our midst and even knocking at the door.

Application

You cannot accept the Kingdom without reform. You have to put things in order. Seek Jesus. Seek the Kingdom. Receive His gift. Then you will want to reform your life.

"Come after me and I will make you fishers of men." (V-19)

Thought

What an invitation? To be called directly by Jesus to walk with Him. No wonder they immediately left their nets. They didn't understand all that was ahead. It was mercifully hidden from their eyes. They just followed along.

Application

You too are called by Jesus. In Baptism, He made you His own. He calls you now. Often you can't hear His words. The modern world pours thousands of words into your ears this day. It uses radio, television, and the latest news. Find a place where these words are shut out. In the quiet, you will begin to hear Jesus.

He called them, and immediately they abandoned boat and father to follow him. (V-22)

Thought

They didn't understand all that was ahead. They heard the call and followed. It was as simple as that. Later, everything would be revealed. Later, they would make other important decisions. For now, they were being asked only to follow along.

Application

Take the first step. Hear Jesus' voice. Discern God's will within yourself. If He is calling, then leave everything you have and follow Him. You cannot find yourself in your natural father's boat. Life begins there. Jesus' call takes you out of that boat and makes you a fisherman somewhere else.

He taught in their synagogues, proclaimed the good news of the kingdom, and cured the people of every disease and illness. (V-23)

Thought

The proclaiming and the curing go together. Cures from every disease and illness follow a proclaiming of the Kingdom. People have their eyes opened. They understand the Father's love and are prepared for God's touch.

Application

Are your eyes closed? Reading these gospels should open the mystery to you. If you have any disease or illness, submit it to the healing power of the gospel. As you read these words, let the power of Jesus be released.

They carried to him all those afflicted with various diseases and racked with pain. (V-24)

Thought

During His mortal life, the power of Jesus worked through His physical body. This body was limited to one place, so that the afflicted had to be carried to wherever He was.

Now, He is risen from the dead. His immortal, risen body is no longer limited by space and time. So, when He says, "I am with you," it is true.

Application

Receiving the gift of Jesus is no longer a question of place or geography. It is no longer a question of going somewhere to find Jesus. He is already right where you are now. Don't move. Just believe and ask.

CHAPTER 9
THE BLESSED ONES (5:1-12)

His disciples gathered around him, and he began to teach them: (V-1&2)

Thought

Jesus, that incomprehensible Word equal to the Father, speaks human words for all to understand. He uses the same human words we do. His words can be heard and understood. What a gift to have the Word as a teacher!

Application

Jesus wants to teach you today. In every event, even those that seem to go wrong. He teaches you. In your heart, Jesus speaks. His words are simple, easy to understand. Listen.

"...the reign of God is theirs..." (V-3)

Thought

When is a man truly rich? When he has God's riches. Here, Jesus promises the poor in spirit the whole reign of God, especially the protection of the Father.

Application

Where is your heart? What does it seek today? You are supposed to seek first the Kingdom and then the secondary things will be added. You can excuse yourself. Today you are too busy. Today has to be given over to some important matters. Will you be better prepared to seek the Kingdom tomorrow, if you don't seek it today?

"...Blest too are the sorrowing;..." (V-4)

Thought

People don't want sorrows. They run from them. They pretend they will never happen. They are never ready for sorrows. They have no means to prepare. The Kingdom is different. As the body releases chemicals in times of fear or danger, Jesus promises a stream of consolations in our sorrows.

Application

What do you do when sorrow comes? Drink? Blame yourself? Go back over the details? Blot it out of your mind? Escape into your work? Or do you turn to Jesus who wants to console you in every sorrow even those you caused for yourself.

"...Blest are they who hunger and thirst for holiness;..." (V-6)

Thought

The world hungers and thirsts but not for holiness. Usually it is for the world's goods, or power, or acclaim. All of life is a choice. To the little ones have been revealed the mysteries of the Kingdom. They will not waste their time on false choices. Jesus, alone, is the center of their decisions.

Application

How do you choose? What enters into your decisions? Are your criteria all mixed up? Does confusion reign? What seems important to you today is discarded tomorrow. You will always need a new direction, unless from the beginning you hungered and thirsted for holiness.

"...Blest too the peacemakers;..." (V-9)

Thought

What a thankless task, trying to bring warring parties to the peace table. Is a peacemaker ever thanked? Frequently, the warring parties feel they have done him the favor. Yet someone has to stand up for God's interest. Someone has to save the warring parties from their own blindness.

Application

Are you a peacemaker, a warring party, or a neutral? Do you say, "That is their problem," always excusing yourself from being involved? Sometimes, God wants to draw you into the peacemaker's role. If so, assume that thankless task. You will help people to be set free.

"...Be glad and rejoice, for your reward is great in heaven...." (V-12)

Thought

This whole reading makes no sense unless there is a heaven. But then life itself, the whole world and all of human history make no sense unless there is a heaven. Jesus has no illusions about trying to make earth into a heaven. Earth is extremely important only because the Kingdom of heaven is at hand.

Application

What do you rejoice in? Answering that question will reveal your heart to you. Examine yourself today. If you rejoice in the wrong things, your heart needs to be changed. If you rejoice in the right things, then the Kingdom is yours.

CHAPTER 10
SALT AND LIGHT (5:13-20)

"You are the salt of the earth." (V-13)

Thought

Salt preserves and gives taste. It claims nothing for itself. It acts upon whatever food it is placed in. It serves both the owner and the food, a symbol of selfless giving.

Application

God has some work for you today. Jesus has told you your vocation. You are the salt of the earth! You will choose today whether or not you will actually be that salt. The next part presents the problem.

"...what if salt goes flat?..." (V-13)

Thought

It is a powerless salt, unable to serve either the master or the food. Fit only to be cast aside. A person who is true salt glorifies God, serves others and is not cast out as useless.

Application

Stop wondering about your life. Place yourself in the Master's hands. Believe in the call of your Baptism. Learn what is needed to be true salt. Seek others whose gifts can preserve you. If you want to be the salt of the earth, Jesus can use you.

"You are the light of the world..." (V-14)

Thought

Jesus said this of Himself. Now He says the same of us. In darkness, people stumble, get hurt and certainly cannot move quickly along the road. The first burst of dawn is a welcome sight.

Application

*Without Jesus, every human being walks in darkness.
Without Him, every life is incomplete. Many of those
you met today, do not know Jesus. They don't hear His
word. They don't understand how to come into His
light. That's why He called you also "the light of the
world."*

"...They set it on a stand where it gives light to all in the house..." (V-15)

Thought

In homes, the light is in the ceiling, illuminating
everything in the room. Even a smaller light is on a
table. There is need for wisdom here and also some
boldness. First, to discover the right lampstand and
then to place the lamp there.

Application

*Where is your lampstand? When should you be
speaking up? Don't think you have nothing to say.
Otherwise, those who think and speak only in a worldly
way will grab the lampstand for themselves then
everything will be in darkness.*

"Do not think that I have come to abolish the law and the prophets..." (V-17)

Thought

Some light already exists. Traditional wisdom is stored
in the Church, for all to have. People don't need totally
new light, as if everything was darkness. God has give
His light. We are lights for our time. The former things
shouldn't be cast away.

Application

*You must be a light that is rooted in Jesus, the Church,
and the Scriptures. Let what is past serve you. Don't
be carried away with modern foolishness, as if the past*

31

contains no light. If the new sweeps away all that is old, then much light is destroyed.

"...Whoever fulfills and teaches these commands shall be great in the Kingdom of God." (V-19)

Thought
People can't really teach a command, until they first fulfill it. Otherwise their actions contradict their words. Their words will have a hollow ring. Jesus' commands can't live only on the lips. They must be rooted in the heart.

Application
Jesus' words have power. They can go deeply within. Changes will come about just by reading and praying over the words. Do that today, tomorrow and the next day. Suddenly you will find that you are both fulfilling and teaching these commands.

"...unless your holiness surpasses that of the Scribes and Pharisees you shall not enter the kingdom of God." (V-20)

Thought
When can people say they are holy enough? When can they call themselves faithful servants? To try to measure holiness is a mistake. To stop growing in holiness is an even greater one. Jesus is not a hard taskmaster, driving us constantly on. He just sees that every day is a gift from the Father's hands, giving us a chance to grow in the Kingdom.

Application
This day has been given you by the Father. What will you do with this day? What sights have you set before you? On what course do you intend to steer your ship?

The world calls you to buy and sell. Your own selfishness will drive you in a different direction. But the Spirit has been poured into your heart, so the Kingdom of God can be yours.

CHAPTER 11
THE KINGDOM'S COMMANDS (5:21-32)

"...everyone who grows angry with his brother shall be liable to judgment;..." (V-22)

Thought
"To grow angry" means that the feelings have built up over a time. They have been deliberately fostered, and never repented. No attempt has been made to quell the anger, to see the other person's side or to give the benefit of the doubt. The destructive force of wrath is fed and nourished. It is allowed uncontrolled sway, bringing about blindness and hardness of heart.

Application
You cannot control the emotions that suddenly spring up. They are natural reactions. However, you can determine which feelings are fed and find root in your heart. You can control anger and hostility. You can be open to forgiveness.

"...leave your gift at the altar, go first to be reconciled with your brother, and then come and offer your gift..." (V-24)

Thought
What a powerful mixing of images! A man trying to be one with God through a gift, is told that he isn't ready to be one with God. That door is shut until he opens his heart to his brother. His open door to God isn't enough if other doors are deliberately closed.

33

Application

Are you open to your fellow man? Begin with those closest to you. How can your relationship to them be improved? Among those you meet regularly, to whom are you not reconciled? Is there anyone whom you don't even speak to? Anyone to whom you are deliberately unfair?

"Otherwise your opponent may hand you over to the judge..." (V-25)

Thought

Reconciliation suddenly becomes expedient. We have moved from the altar to the judge. If the religious motive doesn't result in getting people together, then maybe the practical motive will. People need one another, and to be at odds always costs a heavy price.

Application

Are you at odds with others? Are you willing to take the first step toward reconciliation? Are you ready to see that warring and bickering are not the way to go about things? Jesus offers you a whole new vision of human relationships. All is made new for those who hear His word and act on it.

"...anyone who looks lustfully at a woman has already committed adultery with her in his thoughts." (V-28)

Thought

These relationships extend to women and even to thoughts about women. How far is Jesus going to go? When is He going to stop pushing the Kingdom even into our secret thoughts? Why can't He be satisfied with an external Kingdom with outward signs and sacrificial offerings? After all people will be glad to come and offer their gifts at the altar, if they can have their private lives.

Application
Once you have yielded to the Kingdom, nothing is your own. All belongs to Jesus, including your thoughts. His power enters everywhere. Whenever a door is open, He will come!

Give your hopes and thoughts and desires to Him. At first, you will not understand, because so much has to change. Only when you experience His Freedom and new life, will these words be seen as a gift.

"Better to lose part of your body than to have it cast into Gehenna." (V-29)

Thought
Twice Jesus concludes this way. It is difficult for Him to offer two unpleasant options. Yet some people have to tell the truth to others. Doctors have to speak truthfully. Loving parents and teachers have to speak truthfully. So Jesus had to say truthfully that certain acts cause death.

Application
Certain parts of your life are filled with death. Jesus tells you to stay away from them. For some, alcohol; for others, money or power; for others, lust or ambition. Be honest about those parts. Face the problem squarely. Listen to Jesus that they can cause death.

"...everyone who divorces his wife - lewd conduct is a separate case - forces her to commit adultery." (V-32)

Thought
There is no private life for anyone committed to Jesus. That person can't mark any part of his life as "out of bounds," as if that part should not be touched or

changed by the Kingdom. When a person gives his heart to Jesus, everything else is included.

Application
Don't be afraid of the demands. Even the apostles thought some things impossible. See every command of Jesus as new freedom. See every moral teaching as encouragement that Jesus can get you to that point. The Kingdom is for everybody. With every demand, Jesus says, "I'll do that for you, if you'll let me."

CHAPTER 12
THE IMPOSSIBLE COMMANDS
(5:33-48)

"What I tell you is: do not swear at all." (V-34)

Thought
If a man's word is true, he doesn't have to add external proof. If his word is false, swearing just multiplies his lie. Words are important to Jesus, because they flow from the heart. A depraved heart puts forth a polluted stream of words.

Application
You will speak many words this day. Will they all be true? Or will you get yourself into a corner? Will you speak words that cannot stand on their own, so you will swear to get others to believe? That is not Jesus' way.

"Say, `Yes' when you mean `Yes' and `No' when you mean `No'." (V-37)

Thought
Jesus is the Word made flesh. He teaches us how to use words. To Jesus, every word is precious. The same is not true of everyone. People don't value words.

36

People easily flatter others or they berate others. They explain their motives, or ingratiate themselves. Words not only flow from the heart. Once spoken, they change the heart.

Application

It is hard for you to fulfill this command. Your words come so quickly and so freely, like a torrent. They tend to focus on yourself, your interests, helping you to get what you want. Jesus said clearly that the food you eat is not as important as the words you speak.

"...offer no resistance to injury." (V-39)

Thought

The gospel continues to push people far beyond what they can even imagine. Certainly it is fair not to take advantage of others. However, to offer no resistance to injury seems to go too far. Where will this gospel message end? Only at the cross and Calvary.

Application

Don't water this down. Don't say that it has to be interpreted. Today there will be moments of injury. Words will be unjustly spoken against you. People will take advantage of you. If you spend the whole day demanding that you get fairly treated on every occasion, you have no energy left to seek the Kingdom.

"Should anyone press you into service for one mile, go with him two miles." (V-41)

Thought

What if no one was thoughtful? What if no one was able to put aside his present needs for others? Only the strong and powerful could survive.

Application
Today you will have many chances "to go the extra mile." If you do, than a new bond will exist between you and the other. Maybe, the person has never been helped before. Maybe they have never trusted anyone. Maybe they have never said a true "thank you." God's work will begin when you have finished your extra mile.

"My command to you is: love your enemies, pray for your persecutors." (V-44)

Thought
Jesus reverses everything. He turns the whole world upside down. All worldly wisdom is being destroyed and turned to foolishness. Jesus has a better way of our relating to one another. He knows that the world's way has only generated wars and starvation and death.

Application
You have enemies and persecutors. Don't even ask yourself just who is right and who is wrong. Answering that is useless. Unraveling the past is useless. Today, just love your enemies and pray for your persecutors.

"If you love those who love you, what merit is there in that?" (V-46)

Thought
The command is puzzling. The reasoning makes sense. Loving those who love you and greeting those who greet you is a normal human response. People would do that even if Jesus never lived. The Kingdom asks people to act beyond what they grasp by reason.

Application
Do you think and judge on a human level? Do you do something only if it makes sense to you? Jesus says

that it is not enough. He asks faith from you. Only faith will open your heart and allow something new to begin.

"In a word, you must be made perfect as your heavenly Father is perfect." (V-48)

Thought
The most impossible ideal of all! When is Jesus going to learn that we are only human beings? When is He going to leave us alone and say that we have already accomplished a lot?

Application
Today you must hear this word. All that you have done so far, is as nothing to what God will work in you today. The Kingdom is coming. Jesus' action inside you is quickly multiplying, don't stop now. Jesus wants to make you perfect as His heavenly Father.

CHAPTER 13
PRAYING TO THE FATHER (6:1-15)

"Otherwise expect no recompense from your heavenly Father." (V-1)

Thought
Jesus always kept His eyes on the Father. Everything was judged by how the Father judged. From the very beginning Jesus was about His Father's business. At the end, He commended his Spirit to His Father.

Application
Don't just rush headlong through this day. The Father gave you this day. Keep your eyes on Him. Make decisions realizing He is close. The Father sees every deed and generously rewards even the smallest acts done for Him.

"Whenever you pray, go to your room, close your door, and pray to your Father in private." (V-6)

Thought

This prayer safeguards purity of intention. The Father relationship dominates this prayer. It is not mixed with social or political rewards. The person who prays in secret knows he is serious about his Father-relationship. Closing the door behind represents a definite committal.

Application

How often do you pray in quiet? Do you seek even just a few minutes to close the door? They are important moments. They need not be long but they should be every day.

"...your kingdom come, your will be done on earth as it is in heaven." (V-10)

Thought

The Father's interests dominate the first half of this prayer. People are supposed to rejoice that God is glorified and listened to. Unfortunately, people's thoughts, even their prayers, begin and end with themselves. A serious change is needed.

Application

If you are going to catch on to this idea of living with God, much has to change. You even have to approach God differently. He comes first. He doesn't come second or third. He definitely is not someone you get around to from time to time.

"...Give us today our daily bread." (V-11)

Thought

God knows what people need. He always provides for them. People are the ones who are one-sided. They concentrate on their own well being.

Application

This is a new world for you. Instead of always thinking of yourself, you now think of God. Instead of providing for yourself, you realize that God provides for those who praise His name. How can you get to think that way? Just come each day into the Father's presence.

"...Subject us not to the trial but deliver us from the evil one..." (V-13)

Thought

Poor mankind. It is subjected to so many trials, sufferings and, besides all that, the evil one. However, everything can be used. Weakness can be the door to the Kingdom. Disappointment can lead the child to his father. Sufferings led the Prodigal Son to return. Trials remind people that they need the Father's protection.

Application

How do you see your trials and sufferings, and sorrows? Your natural response is discouragement. Start seeing trials in a different light. Without disappointment and trials, you might wander from the Father and get lost forever.

"...If you forgive the faults of others, your heavenly Father will forgive you yours." (V-14)

Thought

That is a great rate of exchange! Who cannot trust Jesus that He will fulfill the promise. Our small deeds of forgiveness release God's forgiveness.

Application
Who has hurt you? Who has deceived you? Destroyed you? Vilified you? Closed doors to you? Overlooked you? You think you have much to forgive. Look at your own faults, known and unknown. All of these will be wiped out by the Heavenly Father.

CHAPTER 14
THE CORRECT TREASURE (6:16-25)

"I assure you, they are already repaid." (V-16)

Thought
What a poor reward for all the trouble caused by fasting! Yet the opinions of men are valueless. Truly important is what the heavenly Father thinks.

Application
What others think of you constantly exerts it's power over you. Don't bother with human opinion. If you do, it will quickly ruin you. Be concerned only about the Heavenly Father's opinion.

"...and your Father who sees what is hidden will repay you." (V-18)

Thought
Scripture speaks of two hidden things, the hidden evil works of darkness and the hidden good works. Evil is hidden to avoid detection. The good is hidden to preserve the heavenly reward.

Application
What do you hide? Do you trumpet your good works and cover up your evil deeds? You should hide your good works. Your evil deeds you should expose to the priest who can forgive and cleanse.

"Do not lay up for yourselves an earthly treasure." (V-19)

Thought

People need to hear these words everyday. As the sun rises, they start off on human pursuits, heading into the market place to gain their earthly treasure. What else is the day for, they think, except to store-up earthly treasure?

Application

How do you face this day? What feelings throb in your heart? What are your goals? Why do you seek them? To what lengths are you willing to go? Does it matter who gets hurt in the process? Your earthly treasure isn't the Kingdom, so don't make it your god.

"Moths and rust corrode: thieves break in and steal." (V-19)

Thought

Seeking an earthly treasury seems like wisdom. It looks like the smart thing to do. But a second glance uncovers the foolishness. Things wear out. The body only needs so many sets of clothes or shoes. The final question about wealth always is, "who will inherit it after death?" Earthly wealth is a very passing treasure, not at all to be valued as the world sees it.

Application

You need a new understanding. You must have a whole new way of thinking. You need a conversion. What you thought was important, really isn't. How could you be so wrong? Because you listened, like everyone else, to what the world told you. Listen now, to Jesus.

"Make it your practice instead to store up heavenly treasure..." (V-20)

Thought

This is not a short-term deed. It is not the work of one day or week. It's not just a good resolution people hope to keep. Jesus says, "Make it your practice." How much human wealth would a person have if he saved every day? "Storing up heavenly treasure" should be a daily practice.

Application

You need a new orientation, a whole different direction. You have been saving the wrong currency. You have gathered the worthless dollars of this world. Let Jesus turn you around. Let go of some money. Give it to the hungry of the world. Let go of some time. Give it to your loved ones. What you give away, Jesus gathers up. What you cling to, rusts in your grasp.

"Remember, where your treasure is, there your heart is also." (V-21)

Thought

A lifetime of wisdom in one saying! It isn't that difficult for someone to read his own heart. The person merely looks at where he spends his time, his money and his energy. If he examines his life and feelings he can answer the question, "What do I treasure?" The second question would be "Is this what I should be treasuring?"

Application

What do you value? What are you willing to pay a price for? Are they the same things the world values? As you ask those questions, move on to that final question, "Why did God make me? Why do I exist?" Asking those questions will direct you to Jesus.

"No man can serve two masters." (V-24)

Thought

This saying is a warning. People want Jesus to be their Master. They also seem to enjoy having other masters. They delude themselves that serving many masters doesn't really ruin Jesus' rule.

Application

In theory, you can see the foolishness of serving many masters. In practice you have many masters. The other masters seem close. They offer many things right now. Jesus seems so far. Just remember that the Kingdom is at hand. Recall how free you were when you served Him alone.

CHAPTER 15
THE FATHER'S WISDOM (6:26-34)

"Look at the birds in the sky. They do not sow or reap, they gather nothing into barns; yet your heavenly Father feeds them." (V-26)

Thought

"Free as a bird" summarizes the human feeling upon seeing creatures able to soar to the heavens. Nature has provided for them. They are above the struggle for existence experienced by other animals, including man.

Application

Look at your worries and cares. How much do they limit you? How much do you allow them to overcome you? Other people, with much heavier burdens, seem to manage. The secret is the heavenly Father. Do you know He wants to help? Do you know what he can do?

"Learn a lesson from the way the wild flowers grow." (V-28)

Thought

How do the wild flowers grow? The seed contains everything. The flower's beauty is already contained in its very beginning. The seed takes advantage of where the wind scatters it.

Application

God has already put gifts within you. You have human talents. Also, you have Jesus, who gladly shares with you His own Spirit. Where has God planted you? Where do you live and work? Like a wild flower, begin there. Don't wait. Don't say the circumstances are not right. Learn from the wild flowers.

"...will he not provide much more for you, O weak in faith!" (V-30)

Thought

How much will God provide? Who is to say? Nature scatters millions of seeds, knowing only a few will ever flower. That's how God clothes the grass.

Application

If God is prodigal in nature, how much will He spend on you? Do you experience that love? Do you see any results from that love? First, you have to believe. Then you will experience God's generosity.

"Stop worrying, then, over questions like, `What are we to eat, or what are we to drink, or what are we to wear?'" (V-31)

Thought

Every day has its questions. Jesus never said there were no questions. He said that today shouldn't be wasted on the wrong questions. While we worry over what to eat or drink or wear, the important questions go unanswered. Wisdom begins by asking the right questions.

Application
The questions you ask yourself today depends on where your heart is. You have one set of questions. God has another. Let God give you His questions for today. They will unlock the mystery of why God made you.

"The unbelievers are always running after these things." (V-32)

Thought
"Chasing butterflies!" That's how people describe a senseless search. Butterflies are difficult to catch and little is gained. Yet everything on earth is more passing than the fastest butterfly. Fame, money, position and power are sought so eagerly yet pass so quickly.

Application
What are you running after? Are you any different than the unbeliever? Do you search for your goals? Or for the poor and the needy?

"Seek first his kingship over you, his way of holiness..." (V-33)

Thought
The true goal is clear. The KING is at hand. His kingdom doesn't pass away. Some actions lead to that Kingdom. The cup of cold water in His name; going the second mile; forgiving injury. The world sees none of these as important. They are God's "way of holiness."

Application

Today has a mystery and you must search. Don't search for what to eat or drink or wear. That is the wrong search. Look for the Kingdom. It's there today - somewhere. When you find the Kingdom, don't let it go. You have found the treasure in the field and the pearl of a great price.

"Enough then of worrying about tomorrow. Let tomorrow take care of itself." (V-34)

Thought

There is no tomorrow. Tomorrow never comes. Tomorrow exists only on calendars and in our minds. Only today exists. Today is precious. It is important, not to be lost. No one has ever found the Kingdom tomorrow. The Kingdom only comes today.

Application

If you see how important is today you are beginning to grasp the Kingdom. If you see today as the Father's gift, you are already seizing the Kingdom. And if you experience the care of the Father, then the Kingdom has come in your midst today.

CHAPTER 16
INTERNAL DISPOSITIONS (7:1-11)

"If you want to avoid judgment, stop passing judgment." (V-1)

Thought

A person measures life by his own thoughts. Human nature, left alone, places the individual at the center. Everything centers around the person. If a person wears dark glasses, everything becomes dark. If a person is filled with himself, he sees everyone and everything in a selfish light.

Application

Who are you to judge anyone? You are not God. You do not know the trials, difficulties or motives of others. You have no right to judge. You have no talent to judge. When you judge, you ruin and destroy yourself by your own critical spirit.

"The measure with which you measure will be used to measure you." (V-2)

Thought

The saying goes, "Getting a little of your own medicine." It means receiving the same type of pain the person usually gives to others. The reform asked here is difficult. How many can reflect and realize they are judging others?

Application

Don't be satisfied with surface change. Don't be surprised when Jesus reveals what is in your heart. Realize that you are all twisted and turned inside. You go in so many directions. You can't change your own heart. Only Jesus can. You have to be willing to let it happen

"Remove the plank from your own eye first:..." (V-5)

Thought

At certain times, a position of authority demands that a person speak to another about his deeds. Jesus isn't talking about those occasions. They are painful for the speaker and profitable for the listener. He speaks here of the critical spirit, of the judging spirit, and of the destruction wrought by a harsh tongue.

Application

What spirit is within you? Do you manipulate? Take advantage? Always seek the dominant position? Your heart needs to be changed by Jesus before you dare try to change others.

Yet once changed, you will approach others in a different way. You will truly help them. Your words will be different. Your manner of speaking will build up and not destroy or ruin.

"Do not give what is holy to dogs or toss your pearls before swine." (V-6)

Thought
This verse applies to the Scribes and Pharisees, who refuse to receive the gospel. The gospel is so precious, more valuable than pearls. Their attitude is so poor that preaching the gospel to them is tossing pearls before swine.

Application
If your heart is true, treasure Jesus' gifts. You realize that these gifts; His inspired word, His grace and Eucharist are far greater than your worthiness. Don't trample the gift under your feet. Bend your knee to worship and receive.

"Ask, and you will receive. Seek, and you will find. Knock, and it will be opened to you." (V-7)

Thought
Jesus keeps saying "It is the heart that matters." The heart judges, criticizes, passes verdicts, tramples and tears the gospel to shreds. The heart also asks, seeks, knocks and receives the gospel and eternal life.

Application
Where are you with the gospel of Jesus Christ? Do you see yourself as better than the gospel? Do you see no personal need for the gospel? Or, are you subject to it, obedient to it, and therefore, open to its gift?

50

"...how much more will your heavenly Father give good things to anyone who asks him!" (V-11)

Thought

It's all so logical. Even enemies give good things if harassed by others. Friends give very readily. Relatives are usually quick to share. Where does that put the heavenly Father? Surely, he'll give to any who ask.

Application

But when was the last time you asked? And even more importantly, when was the last time you thought you received? Both should have happened today. Both should happen every day.

You will get better at "asking the Father," if you do it regularly. You will learn what to ask for, how to receive and what you have to do to cooperate. Learning to "ask the Father" is a whole new world.

CHAPTER 17
PERSONAL WISDOM (7:12-23)

"Treat others the way you would have them treat you:..." (V-12)

Thought

This demand is reasonable enough. Heroic deeds aren't sought, just thoughtfulness and sensitivity. It is easy to grieve over hurts received. It is difficult to see that the same hurts have often been afflicted on others. No one has to give away his rights. Everyone is merely asked to respect the same rights in others.

Application

How do you treat the many others in your life? Do you bow lowly to the powerful and then brow beat the helpless? Or, do you walk as a child of God, realizing that the powerful have no claim upon you, while the helpless have many claims upon your charity and thoughtfulness.

"The gate that leads to damnation is wide..." (V-13)

Thought
Damnation is certainly far from our minds. It shouldn't become a daily preoccupation. However, the teaching on possible damnation is necessary at certain definite moments. At times, the person knows clearly that his path is the wrong one. How does a person overcome the temptation to steal or to abort, or to be unfaithful, or to accept a bribe? The person needs to realize that some choices would alienate him from God.

Application
Let this be a time of repentance. Turn away from the wide road that is walked all too easily. Seek out a spiritual guide. Find someone to whom you can present your questions. Don't beat around the bush. Don't walk in darkness when light is available.

"But how narrow is the gate that leads to life, how rough the road, and how few there are who find it!" (V-14)

Thought
This verse could easily discourage. But why do few find the narrow road? Because few are interested in finding. Jesus said that everyone who seeks shall find. The person who seeks the narrow road has already begun to walk it.

Application
Seek the narrow road. When you find it, you'll find Jesus there. It's the road He walked. In fact, He is the

road. Don't look at how narrow the road is. Don't be discouraged by its demands. When you find it and walk it, Jesus will be there.

"Be on your guard against false prophets, who come to you in sheep's clothing but underneath are wolves on the prowl." (V-15)

Thought

People quickly accept a gentle sheep into their midst. They would never do that with a fierce wolf. That's the problem! By not being on guard, people let ideas into their lives that can destroy.

Application

What are the wolves in your life? How did you let them in? For the alcoholic, the words were "One drink won't matter." For the ambitious, the words were "Now you can be great."

Look around your life. What tears you apart? Ruins your peace? Destroys God's work in you? Discern your problems and unmask the wolves in sheep's clothing.

"You can tell a tree by its fruit." (V-20)

Thought

What a big help these words are. Jesus tells us exactly where to look. Don't look at the trunk, or the limbs, or the leaves. Reach up and look at the fruit. What's the tree's final product? What's the result?

Application

St. Paul helps you even more. He lists the bad fruit (Gal. 5:19-21) and the good fruit (Gal. 5:22-23). Reading those lists will help you see clearly what state your life is in.

"None of those who cry out `Lord, Lord,' will enter the kingdom of God..." (V-21)

Thought
Isn't it good to cry out "Lord, Lord?" Really, it means nothing to have the words on the lips and nothing in the heart. That is called "lip service." Having "Lord" on the lips also deceives the person into believing that he has the Lord in his heart.

Application
What is really in your heart? It's not that difficult to answer. Look at your behavior. Where do you spend your time and energy? That tells you what is in your heart. What do you avoid? That tells you what is not in your heart.

"Then I will declare to them solemnly, `I never knew you.'" (V-23)

Thought
Jesus is the Word. He is ever true to the Father. In Him there is no darkness, not even a shadow. Each person is also an image of the Father. Everyone is called to be true with no darkness or shadow.

Application
Who are your models? Whom do you emulate? Whom do you envy? Whom do you wish you were like? Don't you realize that you are the Father's image? Don't spend your time envying others. You have your own worth and your own image. Jesus wants to help you become the true you. He wants to say, "I know you."

CHAPTER 18
JESUS' WORD (7:24-29)

"Anyone who hears my words and puts them into practice is like the wise man who built his house on rock." (V-24)

Thought

After a good speech, people clap. After a presidential talk, commentators analyze his words. The gospel message isn't something people clap for. It is also not something people analyze. The gospel demands a response. That response can't just be "That is a nice message." Jesus' words claim total loyalty. He expects the message to be put into practice.

Application

The gospels give light for every area of life. If you really want to "put them into practice" read the gospels as the advice of a close friend who knows you intimately. When gospel sayings jump off the page at you; when you say over and again "that's me" or "that's my problem," then you are "hearing and putting into practice."

"It did not collapse; it had been solidly set on rock." (V-25)

Thought

The problems of rain, torrents and wind were regular problems in Palestine. The only solution was to find rocky ground to build the house on. Nothing else worked. No matter how deep the foundation or how supposedly well built, the powerful running water from storms would wash away other foundations.

Application

Nothing substitutes for Jesus' word. If you set aside His

word, you have no foundation. Everything in your life will be built upon a shaky foundation. No matter how well you build, or how expensive the materials you use, your life will collapse. First, find the ROCK of Jesus' word. Then, build your life on His word.

"...like the foolish man who built his house on sandy ground." (V-26)

Thought

Children play in the sand. They even delight to watch the waters come and destroy what they have built. They can start again. It's sad, though, when adults build their lives upon sand. How can the person be consoled who sees his life's work ruined? How many times can a person start again?

Application

Examine your life, your work, your family, your friends and your goals. Don't examine them like the world does. Rather, ask yourself if each part is built on Jesus' words.

Perhaps you see very little connection between the gospel and your personal success or failure. As you continually examine those parts, you will see how often you have built upon sandy ground instead of rock.

"It collapsed under all this, and was completely ruined." (V-27)

Thought

Collapses exist everywhere. There have been disgraces in public office, bankruptcies, marital failures, and rupture of children-parent relationships. These are the obvious ones. Some "collapses" are hidden from public view. These are alcoholism, addiction, lying and cheating that indicate a "false life." Other collapses are internal, such as destroyed hope, ruined self-esteem, meaninglessness and depression. Everywhere collapses abound. People should listen to Jesus' words.

Application

Your life doesn't have to collapse. Yet, Jesus says "it will fall apart" if you don't build upon His word. Your life can always survive the good times. It is when the trials of rain and wind come that you need to have His word. When the torrents come, its too late to build or decide. The decision must be made now.

Jesus finished this discourse and left the crowds spellbound at his teaching. (V-28)

Thought

"Being left spellbound" isn't enough. What happened when the spell was broken? Some acted on the word. Their lives were changed. Others forgot the word. They just went about as before.

Religion can become just a passing feeling, a moment of being spellbound. Or religion can be a true, daily way of life.

Application

What do you do with Jesus' word? Do you act on it and let it change you? Or, do you set it aside, like a coat or a dress that you only wear from time to time. Is God's word something you clothe yourself in on occasions, or is His word your daily work habit?

The reason was that he taught with authority... (V-29)

Thought

If people set His word aside, that's their fault. Jesus, Himself, never gave people that option. He never left people in doubt. He taught with authority. Jesus never said people were allowed to set His word aside. A good doctor gives no choice about taking medicine that will save a life.

Application
Someday you will come before Jesus. His word will be clear. You won't miss any portion. Nothing else will exist to confuse you. By then, it should be a familiar word. You should have heard it thousands of times and acted on it. Then Jesus' words will be "Come into My Father's house.

CHAPTER 19
SEEKING CURES (8:1-13)

When he came down from the mountain, great crowds followed him. (V-1)

Thought
There is no secret about the source of Jesus' power. The mountain top prayer symbolizes His relationship to the Father. Jesus preached that everything lasting is rooted in his word. Jesus, Himself, serving or based on personal strength. He always found His strength in the Father.

Application
You, too, can have a relationship to the Father. Jesus wants to bestow that gift. Today, you should go up the mountain. Set aside moments from your earthly concern. Let your heart and mind ascend to God. Through those moments of praying you will know the Father as Jesus did.

"Sir, if you will to do so, you can cure me." (V-2)

Thought

The statement is simple. It covers over many feelings, the bad years of illness and the emotions of someone rejected. The words reveal his hope. He is open to a new power. He is willing even to be rejected again.

Application

Be aware of what sickness does. Sickness spreads from the body to the feelings; from the feelings to the thinking. Soon, everything becomes ill. Let God's healing begin in that part affected last. First, let your mind fill with faith; then your feelings with peace and trust. These two you have some control over. When you have gone that far, don't go backward. Hold your ground. God is then free to heal you in every way, even physically.

"I do will it. Be cured." (V-3)

Thought

Is there ever a time Jesus would not will to cure? Is there ever a time the heavenly Father doesn't will our good? Then why are people not always healed and cured when they cry out? In the gospel, everything is so simple. People ask and it is given. There must have been some power in the physical presence of Jesus that led people to a unique level of faith.

Application

The question here is not your level of faith. Faith itself is a special gift, given at a moment and from above. You can't "generate" that kind of faith. You can't "work yourself up to that faith." You can want and seek and believe. You can say a "prayer of faith" believing that the Father hears.

59

"I will come and cure him." (V-7)

Thought

Jesus doesn't keep His power hidden or in reserve. He knows He has the power. He wants it used for everyone. We conceive of God as sort of "laying back," waiting until people wake Him up with their prayers, as if they stir Him to act by fervent pleas. That is a wrong idea. God acts first. He sends Jesus. Jesus wants to come and cure.

Application

How do you think of God? As far away; difficult to get in touch with; slow to act? Your ideas are inadequate. You can't get new ones by reading theology books. You have to let God act in your life. Then you will see that He's much different than you thought.

"I am not worthy to have you under my roof..." (V-8)

Thought

How did the centurion ever arrive at this idea? He had never met Jesus. His was not a poor home. He heard the stories of Jesus. God worked within his heart, and moved him to ask by constantly bringing those stories to his mind. Because he recalled the stories he had great faith even before meeting Jesus.

Application

You know the stories of Jesus. Do you recall them? Do you allow their power into your life? There's no need to have met the mortal Jesus. You have complete access to Him by faith. Recall the stories and let your faith be stirred.

60

"I assure you, I have never found this much faith in Israel." (V-10)

Thought

With this degree of faith, there's no question that Jesus will act. His power isn't limited to distance. This man, however, is a centurion. He is not even a member of the chosen people.

Application

You don't have to be a "professional religious" to believe. Faith is found everywhere. Faith isn't limited to one class of people. Everyone has access to Jesus. Whatever your state in life, believe.

"Go home. It shall be done because you trusted." (V-13)

Thought

How did the centurion feel on the way home? Jesus had not turned him away. He didn't refuse to talk to him because he wasn't Jewish. Jesus had commended him. He had even wanted to come to his home... The centurion was at peace. His mission accomplished. The full gift awaited him on his return home.

Application

Jesus isn't just someone who gives you a good feeling. He didn't just comfort the man. He didn't just make him feel good about a bad situation. He acted and changed the situation.

Jesus wants to do the same for you. You have a lot of situations that need His power. Bring them to Jesus. Start with your most hopeless problem or the situation that pains you most. Don't give up. Keep seeking until Jesus acts.

CHAPTER 20
HEALINGS AND A CALL (8:14-23)

He took her by the hand and the fever left her. (V-15)

Thought

What happens when a person takes our hand? We feel their strength, support, warmth and reassurance. We respond even though we might be weak. That gift, though, is limited to human help. What's it like to hold Jesus' hand? Divine power is there. God's fullness is present. We are changed and made new.

Application

You are not alone. Jesus won't leave you an orphan. To touch Jesus is to touch God's fullness. The Word is in your midst. Grab His hand and let Jesus change you.

As evening drew on, they brought him many who were possessed. (V-16)

Thought

Why evening? Because the sick couldn't get there by themselves. They depended upon the able-bodied who had tasks during the day. Jesus waits. He doesn't say "why didn't you come during the day?" He understands. This was the earliest they could make it.

Application

Evening is a good time for you to come to Jesus. The day's work is over. Jesus understands that you were busy with your work. He won't complain that you should have come earlier.

Evening also represents the later years of life. Don't stay away from Jesus just because you didn't come to Him earlier in life.

He expelled the spirits by a simple command. (V-16)

Thought

The people were in bondage to fear, anxiety, addictions, hostility, etc. All of these ruin and destroy. There are many "spirits" and their source isn't always known.

TWO TRUTHS ARE CLEAR:
1) Jesus offers us freedom from all bonds.
2) Jesus has power to expel by a simple command.

Application

Ask Jesus to be your Lord. You will then be a slave to no one else and to no other spirit. The prayer is a simple one, "Jesus, be Lord of my day." Jesus takes His Lordship seriously. Since you are now His subject, He will allow no harm to happen to you.

"It was our infirmities he bore, our sufferings he endured." (V-17)

Thought

You and I had no choice about being born. We have no choice about whether or not we will die. For Jesus, both involved a choice. He chose to be born, to suffer and die. The infirmities and sufferings He chose were ours, not His.

Application

The gospel message is a simple one. Jesus loves you and wants to lift many burdens. The burdens He does give you are easy and light. When you invite Him to help you, He will exercise His power to lift your infirmities.

"...but the Son of Man has nowhere to lay his head." (V-20)

Thought
"Nowhere to lay his head" means no resting-place; nowhere to go to be refreshed. The symbol is twofold. Earth really offers no one a true resting-place. No one can stop time. It's foolishness to see anywhere on earth as a resting-place. The second symbol is the importance of Jesus' work. Only limited time remains to accomplish His whole plan.

Application
The gospel challenges you. Is your "busyness" the competitive rush of the world? Do you see God's vision of your tasks upon earth? Do you use your time well? Or are you always seeking "resting places." These "resting places" consume so much of your life that little is accomplished.

"Follow me, and let the dead bury their dead." (V-22)

Thought
Jesus isn't talking about a funeral. He alludes to an aged father whom the son would have to spend many years with before he died.

A right priority exists in this call. God's work has to be done. Constantly putting it off because of other "good reasons," ruins or limits God's power. If the gospel is the "power of God leading everyone who believes in it to salvation..." (Rom. 1:16), then working for the gospel is primary.

64

Application

You are called to work for the gospel. The foundation for this work is your local parish. Offer your services there. Also, find others who want to work for the gospel. Join together. With others helping you won't lose heart.

CHAPTER 21
POWER OVER DISORDERS (8:24-34)

Without warning a violent storm came up on the lake... (V-24)

Thought

At no time, can anyone in this world feel he is perfectly safe. Things happen "without warning." No one knows what today brings, let alone tomorrow or next week.

Application

The world will always disappoint you. It promises a life without storms or trials. The "happy-ever-after" dream is an illusion.

Yet you shouldn't be anxious. The previous verse said that Jesus also got into the boat. Don't trust in a false security but in Jesus who remains with you.

Then he stood up and took the winds and the sea to task. (V-26)

Thought

How can anyone take the winds and the seas to task? They are not rational. They can't even respond to a command as animals do. Everything is under Jesus' control, the food that multiplies and the winds and seas that calm.

Application

If these irrational forces recognize their Creator, shouldn't you? The highest wisdom is to seek Christ's kingship over you. Everything begins with the question "Who controls your life?" If Jesus is your Lord, then everything good is possible. If not, everything tends to get out of order.

"What sort of man is this, they said, that even the winds and the sea obey him?" (V-27)

Thought

That is the central question for everyone. Who is Jesus? What sort of man is He?" A person can answer that question theologically and doctrinally. The real question, though, is "What sort of man is He, for you?" Is He first in your life? Is He everything to you?

Application

It is easy to give the right answer with your lips but have the wrong answer in your heart. Don't keep this truth contained and locked up in a formula. This Jesus, who commands the winds and the sea, is your Lord. He wants to be in command of your life. You, however, are rational and free. Unlike the winds and the sea, you can refuse.

They were possessed by demons and were so savage that no one could travel along that road. (V-28)

Thought

What powers were these that could twist two human beings so that others could not even come near. These powers act like dogs who attack when their privacy is invaded. These two human beings are pictures of what can happen inside every heart. Feelings of isolation from others, of anger, hatred, and jealousy invade and take over.

Application

You, too, can be subject to the same powers. You don't experience their extreme degree, but the same problems are within you.

You can be defensive, not allowing people into your life. The truth is that you don't have to be subject to those feelings. Jesus can set you free.

"Out with you!" (V-32)

Thought

All powers are subject to Jesus. He said that the Father has given Him all authority in heaven and on earth. He has fought the battle with darkness. At His death He triumphed. His victory is ours.

Application

Does Jesus have full authority over you? Or do you keep a part of your life away from Him? If you have never surrendered that part, His power to cast out evil from you is limited. That part remains unredeemed. Surrender everything and receive the complete victory.

The whole herd went rushing down the bluff into the sea and were drowned. (V-32)

Thought

To us this seems a strange story, something out of an eerie mystery novel. The story shows these powers are real. They are not just something in a man's mind. They are not just mental illness that can be cured by medicine. The story teaches us to stay away from the occult powers that we do not understand.

Application

What books do you read? Are you fascinated by the novels with preternatural stories? Do you engage in games, such as tarot cards, Ouija boards, white magic, seances, and astral projections? Do you delve into that whole "twilight zone" of the occult? Get away from them or else you might find yourself with serious problems.

They begged him to leave their neighborhood. (V-34)

Thought

Probably they thought that Jesus, who had just cast out the demons, was a higher demon who had power over the lower. Anyone who had such power was dangerous.

They saw only the external power. They didn't give themselves a chance to really know Jesus. If they did, they would realize that no evil resided in Him.

Application

Give yourself a chance to know Jesus. Don't judge Him by externals or by events that have happened to you. Don't attribute destruction or ruin to Him. In Him is life, not death, for all who believe.

CHAPTER 22
FORGIVING AND CALLING (9:1-13)

"have courage, son, your sins are forgiven." (V-2)

Thought

We come to the high point of Jesus' power. He removes sin. He reaches into a person's memories and his soul. He blots out what now mars them. He set him right with the Father. The Church has always said that this forgiveness is not just an external covering-over, but a true, internal change.

68

Application

This forgiveness is available to you. Do you take it for granted? Do long periods intervene between your use of the sacrament of reconciliation? Do you ever use the sacrament as an excuse for allowing sin to have power over you?

"Why do you harbor evil thoughts?" (V-4)

Thought

Jesus shows them many signs and wonders. They still do not believe. They still test and probe Jesus. They are not yet convinced that he is sent by the Father. They believe He is a passing phenomenon, a charlatan using tricks to lead astray. Jesus remains patient with them. He gives them yet another sign.

Application

Do you still hold back your belief? How many signs has Jesus worked in your midst? You have probably forgotten many of them.

How many signs do you need? Are 100 signs enough? If not, how about a 1000? Really, all the signs in the world can't force you to say "I believe."

"Stand up! Roll up your mat, and go home." (V-6)

Thought

To the demons Jesus says, "out with you." To the paralytic he says, "Stand up!" The demons have made their choice. They will have no part of Jesus. Poor mankind is still choosing. Even in our most powerless moments, when everything seems against us, we can still choose Jesus.

Application

You are often powerless. You are subject to many ills. You are weak in the face of many forces. You have one power. You can choose Jesus. Until the last breath, you can choose Him. Don't wait. Choose Him now.

At the sight, a feeling of awe came over the crowd. (V-8)

Thought

Jesus had forgiven sins. He now proved He had forgiven sins. This is no demonic power. This is no special human power. This is God's power. Jesus controls everything - wind, sea, demons and sin.

Application

How much more do you need to be convinced? Do you need more miracles? They are recorded in the next verses. Do you need more signs? They will be given. But even now, God touches your heart. Say, "I believe! Come Lord Jesus!

He said to him "Follow me." (V-9)

Thought

A very simple sentence. Two words. No explanation and no reasons. Matthew understood what was being offered. He could leave behind the odious job of tax collector and join Jesus in proclaiming the Kingdom. He went from a public sinner to an apostle of God's Kingdom in two words.

Application

Jesus speaks to you. If in any way you have opened your heart, He is speaking to you. What words does He speak? Probably the same one He spoke to someone in Matthew's gospel. Listen. They will be simple words but you will understand.

Jesus was at table
in Matthew's home. (V-10)

Thought

Having come to Matthew, Jesus can now come to his family and friends. When a door is opened Jesus doesn't hesitate. He doesn't worry about criticism. Isn't He the Good Shepherd who goes after the sheep? Jesus Himself said He was the physician who gladly makes house calls.

Application

You certainly want everything good for your family, your loved ones, your friends and neighbors. Especially you want your children to be close to Jesus.

Well, you are the door. Let Jesus come to you in His power. He will then have a greater chance to care for your loved ones.

"I have come to call, not the
self-righteous, but sinners." (V-13)

Thought

Jesus turns everyone's thinking upside down. He seems to be going to the wrong people. He is like an actor who sits in the audience instead of being on stage.

Application

Don't let anything keep you from Jesus. Don't think you have to climb mountains to find Him. Don't imagine that He is open only to the good. Anyone, at anytime, can grasp Jesus. Don't wait to change your life before seeking Him. Seek Jesus first. He will change your life

CHAPTER 23
NEW POWER AND NEW LIFE (9:14-26)

"how can wedding guests go in mourning so long as the groom is with them?..." (V-15)

Thought

These words don't mean only the mortal life of Jesus. They apply now for He is still with us. The wedding symbolizes the Kingdom that has already begun in our midst. Never again can sorrow or despondency conquer the world. Jesus has come and remains.

Application

Realize the Kingdom is always present. Know that you share in Jesus' Risen Life. Do not go about in

mourning. The Bridegroom and the wedding banquet are in your midst.

"Nobody sews a piece of unshrunken cloth on an old cloak;..." (V-16)

Thought

These little sayings are radical statements by Jesus. His teachings are not just to be added to the Old Testament. He is not just another teacher, nor the latest prophet. He brings something new. His life and teachings are not just an evolution from the Old Testament. Such a view will be broken open just as old wineskins are by new wine.

Application

Jesus gives you a new wine. He demands from you a new heart and a new direction. You can't just add Jesus to your life. You need a new heart to contain His gift.

You can't have Jesus and an unchanged life. The whole fabric of your life will break open. When Jesus comes, He makes everything new. All is changed!

"My daughter has just died..." (V-18)

Thought

Five words are unlike any others. Those five are - father, mother, spouse, son and daughter. These words symbolize a unique linking between persons. They are primary. The first two give birth. The third cooperates in birth. The last two are products of birth. What is it like to say, "My daughter has just died?" The sentence is a monument to the emptiness a human being can experience.

Application

In this emptiness, the synagogue leader turned to the right person. In your emptiness, to whom or to what do you turn? You might say, "Well, Jesus happened to be nearby." Don't you know that Jesus is right here, also? By the power of His resurrection He is everywhere. You are always able to turn to Him.

"If only I can touch his cloak," she thought, "I shall get well." (V-21)

Thought

In the shoving and pushing of the crowd, many touched Jesus. This woman touched Jesus in faith. Later, others would touch His hands and feet. Some nailed Jesus to a cross. Thomas would touch the nail prints and the wound. This woman touched in faith and got well.

Application
Each day changes you. You will be quite different tonight than you were this morning. You will either have grown in faith, or the faith you had will be covered over by the cares and the anxieties of the day. You have to ask for faith and take time to nourish faith by prayer. If you do, then special moments of God's gifts will come regularly when you will touch Jesus and be healed.

"Leave, all of you! The little girl is not dead. She is asleep." At this they began to ridicule him. (V-24)

Thought
Their attitudes would have limited Jesus' power (as mysteriously happened at Nazareth). Certainly they were unworthy to witness His power. Miracles, to Jesus, were never a sideshow. They often were not even to be talked about. They were, however, the normal result of faith in the Kingdom. The Kingdom and healings should go together.

Application
Don't be afraid of miracles and healings. God intervenes regularly. He acts more often than you think. Seek His power in the right spirit and you will witness His wonders.

He entered and took her by the hand, and the little girl got up. (V-25)

Thought
The contrast is striking. Jesus just takes the girl's hand and the overwhelming power of being raised from the dead is given. At creation, God just spoke a word and it all began. Nothing is impossible to Him.

74

Application

What can God do with you? Anything. Just by His word, He can raise you out of sinful depths. By the simplest touch of His Spirit, He can put you on the right path. Does He want to change you? That's why He sent Jesus. Let God take your hand, He will quickly raise you up.

CHAPTER 24
HAVING PITY EVERYWHERE (9:27-38)

"Son of David, have pity on us!" (V-27)

Thought

To us the name "Jesus" means more than "David." At this point, however, the two blind men were using the best phrase they knew. They didn't have full knowledge of Jesus, but they didn't let their ignorance keep them from crying out.

Application

Theories about Jesus are not saving events. Salvation doesn't come to you through a head full of theology. The Kingdom comes by putting what you know into practice.

Don't wait for a theology course. You already know Jesus. You know the gospel stories of His power. Cry out the best you can.

When he got to the house, the blind man caught up with him. (V-28)

Thought

Jesus always knew where they were. He wasn't leaving them behind. He was caught up in the crowd, giving His attention to one person at a time.

75

Application

Jesus always knows where you are. In the darkest hours, He is there. When you feel left behind, abandoned so to speak, He is right there. No longer is He even caught up in the crowd. He gives you His full and undivided attention, as a child of His Father.

...and they recovered their sight. (V-30)

Thought

That's the perfect gift for blind men. Just what they needed. With the gift came many new responsibilities. Now they had to work, to help others and especially to tell the story of Jesus to all. With the gift they had to adjust, to relate differently, to take their place in society.

Application

What is your perfect gift? What exact power to you need? Maybe you are asking for the wrong gift? Or maybe you aren't willing to accept the responsibilities that come with the perfect gift?

If you are ready to serve others and if you're willing to tell the story of Jesus to all, His gifts are yours.

once the demon was expelled the mute began to speak. (V-33)

Thought

The mute's faculties were gripped by a higher power. Some question this reality. They deny a world of demons. Others attribute these stories to cultural expressions or to a poor understanding of mental illness. A complete scriptural picture just won't permit that understanding. Scripture, speaking often and in many ways, teaches the reality of evil powers.

Application

This power of evil can touch you. If so, there is a bondage. Your natural faculties are limited. You don't have the extraordinary difficulty of the mute, but other problems can exist. Instead of acting freely, you are limited by fears.

Let Jesus remove these problems so you can freely exercise the powers of God's child.

"Nothing like this has ever been seen in Israel" (V-33)

Thought

Israel was the chosen nation where God's power was regularly manifested. Possibly Israel got used to God. Set limits on His actions. The great actions through Moses and the prophets had happened centuries ago. Nothing was expected to happen now.

Application

You heard of Jesus years ago. You probably have practiced some religion. Maybe God had never surprised you in the past. You don't expect Him to surprise you now.

Don't think that way. Anything can come from God's hand. Expect everything you need. Ask for whatever seems impossible.

Jesus continued his tour of all the towns and villages. (V-25)

Thought

The Father sent Jesus. When He came, Jesus didn't stay in Nazareth announcing that anyone could come and see Him. (No appointment needed?) He is active like the Father. Having come into the world, He goes to every town and village. He doesn't want to miss a single person.

Application
You might see yourself as unimportant; as just a name in the telephone book. You are not that to Jesus. You are everything to Him. He will come to your village; to your home; to your heart.

He taught in their synagogues, he proclaimed the good news of God's reign, and he cured every sickness and disease. (V-35)

Thought
It's important to understand those three activities. Jesus starts with a clear teaching that people in synagogues are used to. Then He proclaims that the teaching is happening. God's reign is present now. When the people allowed Jesus to bestow a faith in His power, he could then cure every sickness and disease.

Application
You believe in a God. You believe in a Jesus who lived 2000 years ago. Do you believe that He is in your midst and that His Kingdom has come upon you? If you do, then let Jesus cure every sickness and disease

CHAPTER 25
THE FIRST MISSIONARIES (10:1-10)

Then he summoned his twelve disciples and gave them authority (V-1)

Thought

Even during His mortal life, Jesus shared the task of salvation. He saw the many who needed the gospel (the harvest) and others who were willing to share His tasks (the laborers).

Jesus didn't keep things to Himself. He shared everything. He shared authority, His tasks, and His power. This sharing took on a new dimension when He went to the Father. He gave everything over to men, including care for the Church.

Application

Jesus wants to share everything with you. How much does He actually share? That depends on you. If you are faithful today, He will share more tomorrow. If you use His power and authority to live and spread the gospel, more will be given.

The names of the twelve apostles are these: (V-2)

Thought

By themselves, these men were just names. Together, they were the special Twelve. St. Paul wrote that these apostles were not wise, nor skilled as the world judges. The people who knew these men, probably weren't overwhelmed. Two qualities, though, set them apart. They are given God's power and, together, they are the "Twelve."

Application

You are called to spread the gospel. You need two powers. The first comes by Jesus sending the Spirit into your heart. The second comes by your joining with others. Look for these others who will join with you in spreading Jesus' word.

"Do not visit pagan territory and do not not enter a Samaritan town..." (V-5)

Thought

Jesus had reasons for these commands. The pagans and Samaritans were not prepared. The time couldn't be wasted. Also, the apostles would grow discouraged by failure. Thirdly, the task was already clear. The Kingdom had to be preached first to the Jews.

Application

You have obvious tasks and responsibility, - the work at hand; the care for your family; the legitimate demands upon your time.
No need to go far afield. No need to burden yourself with more than is possible. Just do your clearly defined tasks well.

"As you go, make this announcement: The reign of God is at hand!" (V-7)

Thought

That's certainly not a complicated message. Anyone can preach it. Everyone can understand it. When that message is preached and accepted, God's power reigns. The truth of God's reign being at hand stirs faith. The next question is "What do I do now?"

Application

Believe that God's reign is already upon you. You don't have to search; nor go any place to find. His reign is at hand! His kingship over you already exists. This gospel preaching just tells you what already is. Accept the message.

The gift you have received, give as a gift. (V-8)

Thought
In His Kingdom, no money passes hands. No bribes; no buying higher places. The rich and the poor mingle as one. All possess everything, because all have received as a gift. All give freely.

In this, the Kingdom and the world clash. Giving as a gift is heresy to the world. The world knows only costs and payments. Nothing is a gift. Everything has a string attached. No wonder the world cannot free anyone.

Application
Try to understand how to "give as a gift." Leave aside the world's ways. You have learned those ways so well they are ingrained. Let go of your grasp on people and possessions. You will freely receive and freely give.

Provide yourselves with neither gold nor silver nor copper in your belts..." (V-9)

Thought
With money in their belts, the apostles could eat and sleep whether they preached the gospel or not. Bringing money along also deprived the people of using the charism of hospitality (Rom. 12:13). It would seriously harm the Apostles' credibility in preaching trust in the Father's riches.

Application
Sometimes God asks you to do a work. Don't think first of what money you can give. Your time, energy and

devotion to the task are the important parts. At other times, God asks you to provide hospitality: to offer your money, your food, and your physical means to those who are preaching the gospel. Respond quickly and completely to both requests.

"The workman, after all, is worth his keep." (V-10)

Thought
These Scriptures give guidelines for Church workers. This simple sentence teaches the right to a fair wage; the need to support gospel workers; the duties of those people who receive the good news; the need for gospel preachers to fulfill their tasks.

Application
If you preach the gospel, you have a right to your keep. This guaranteed life style is yours only if you preach the gospel.

If you receive the gospel message, you should support, not only those teaching you but the evangelizing missionaries of your church who bring the gospel to others.

CHAPTER 26
ADVICE FOR THE MISSIONARIES
(10:11-20)

"...and stay with him until you leave." (V-11)

Thought

The Lord provides for his preachers, but He doesn't cater to their every whim. The preacher should be content with the necessities, not asking his hosts to go to extremes, and not offending them by changing residences.

The generosity of American Catholics toward their Church has provided a whole system of rectories and convents. Today, this gospel seems to be fulfilled by a correct use of Church offerings.

Applications

Set aside a fair and ever generous portion for your parish. Besides that, keep your home available. A welcome home often relieves a person's loneliness. It is a place where people can seek good advice, be cheered up and prepared to face tomorrow's difficulties.

"As you enter his home bless it." (V-12)

Thought

A home isn't formed just by the family members. Guests play a special role. Some people are unworthy to be guests in the home. They bring to the home a disorder. Others bring a blessing. Their stories, their goodness, their worlds of experience bless the family members. Besides, welcoming God's guests brings a special blessing.

Application

Whom do you welcome into your home. Whom do you exclude? Hospitality is a service that returns blessing a hundred-fold. Don't close your doors unless you must. Find time for the person who might need a place of refreshment.

"If anyone does not receive you or listen to what you have to say..." (V-14)

Thought

This is a serious question. Sometimes people do not respond to the gospel. When the preacher has done his work, when he has proclaimed the reign of God, the listener must respond. The Word of God is a seed that must be willingly received.

Application

How do you respond to God's Word? Do you receive the word like a field receives rain, allowing God's power to soak in? Or do you receive the word as cement receives rain, with resistance and no lasting results?

"What I am doing is sending you out like sheep among wolves. You must be clever as snakes and innocent as doves." (V-16)

Thought

Jesus cleverly uses the different qualities associated with four animals to prepare the apostles. Since Jesus cannot accompany them, He prepares them as well as possible. Through these images, Jesus' power will be with them in many different situations.

Application

Jesus prepares you by His words. As you read Matthew's gospel, Jesus' words are placed within you.

He prepares you for many different situations. Read His words daily.

"They will haul you into court, they will flog you in their synagogues." (V-17)

Thought

By the time the gospel was written, these prophecies had already occurred. From the beginning, the apostles were beaten (and were able to rejoice). They weren't preaching a popular message. They challenged evil and darkness. At times they had a full-scale war on their hands.

Application

Even within yourself, the struggle goes on. Certain parts of you resist the gospel message. Certain parts don't want to surrender to the Lordship of Jesus. In this battle, Jesus and His gospels claim their victory over you.

"You will be brought to trial before rulers and kings." (V-18)

Thought

Rulers and kings are symbols of people or situations that seem to have great power. Yet, their ruling dominion is totally external. Only Jesus rules within. The person who inwardly wants Jesus as Lord, does not fear kings and rulers who exercise only external control.

Application

Let Jesus come to you. You will fear no one and no situation. Who can take away your riches and even your life, when you have already given them away to Jesus? No one can rob you, for your treasure is in heaven.

85

"...do not worry about what you will say or how you will say it." (V-19)

Thought

When fear grips the person, especially when he might be called to answer some questions, he tends to review his responses ahead of time. Jesus says that's futile.

Application

If you are doing God's work, walk in truth. If you are doing everything correctly, don't be anxious. Don't worry about what others might ask, or what you will have to say in self-defense. The right words will be yours at that moment.

CHAPTER 27
PROPHESYING THE PERSECUTIONS
(10:21-27)

"Brother will hand over brother to death, and the father his child..." (V-21)

Thought

This, too, had already happened before these words were written. The prophecy was fulfilled in the Jewish households, as the claims of Jesus split the family between believers and non-believers.

Why shouldn't only good come from gospel preaching? Why so many unwanted side effects? Because the gospel is preached to people who are under the powers of sin, evil and darkness. Self-interest and confusion constantly war against the gospel message.

Application

When you accept the gospel, be ready for trials. They will come from within and without. They will come even from family members who should be encouraging you. In our sinful world, even childbirth has its pain. When, however, the pain is past and the child is born, all can rejoice.

"You will be hated by all on account of me." (V-22)

Thought

Why do people hate the good? They themselves do not even know why. By their hatred, they hope to discourage the person. Then, when the person gives up his ideals, they despise and scorn him.

Application

Don't surrender your beliefs to hatred. See the hatred for what it is - a confused response to goodness. Be meek toward those who hate. Try to share with them the very good they envy. You might be surprised by their openness.

"But, whoever holds out till the end will escape death." (V-22)

Thought

Obviously, "escaping death" means eternal life. "Holding out to the end" means until the trial is over. Sometimes the trial ends only with the martyrdom itself.

Jesus' message is constant. He always speaks of His Kingdom not being of this world. He tells us ahead of time not to put our treasures in earthly vessels.

In this world some people escape pain, poverty, hunger or the cold. No one escapes death. Those who have received eternal life in Jesus don't worry about their loss of earthly life.

Application

Rejoice in the promise of Jesus. No need to worry about age or infirmities or anything else that will eventually steal your physical life. Through the gospel message you possess eternal life.

"When they persecute you in one town, flee to the next." (V-23)

Thought

This doesn't sound like the bravest approach possible. Jesus, however, doesn't call his followers to a useless battle. He doesn't seek false martyrs who somehow just enjoy dying. Preaching the gospel involves certain difficulties, possibly even death. But Jesus doesn't teach us to seek out difficulties.

Application

At certain times, you should flee. In some situations you should back off. Be clear about why God called you. Know what He has put you in charge of. Keep your goals clearly in mind. Sometimes you must confront. Other times you should flee.

"The pupil should be glad to become like his teacher, the slave like his master." (V-25)

Thought

Jesus could speak freely about fleeing, about being hated, about being called before kings, and even about death. He experienced them all. He is not an academic teacher who expounds great theories. He lived His words so He could help us live His words.

Application

By becoming familiar with the gospels, you will understand that every situation in your own life had a parallel in the gospels. You will realize you are not alone. The road is familiar. Jesus has already been there.

"Do not let them intimidate you" (V-26)

Thought

Jesus looks at the apostles. He knows what they will face. He knows how weak they are. He knows well the tremendous powers they will oppose. He also knows they will overcome. They can lose only if they begin thinking that the others have greater power. So He warns them, "Don't be intimidated."

Application

Jesus tells you clearly that the victory is yours, but only at the end. You might think you are losing at the beginning, or the middle, or even toward the end. That's not important. Just keep running the race. Don't drop out! He already said that anyone who perseveres to the end automatically wins.

"Nothing is concealed that will not be revealed, and nothing hidden that will not become known." (V-26)

Thought

People perjure, lie, cover-up. They do this so others will not see. Yet, someday everyone will know. People seek out the darkness. They act in hiding so they can get away with their deeds. Yet, someday, everyone will know.

Others give a cup of cold water very quietly. Others pray in the quiet of their rooms. Others give away their treasures silently. Someday, everyone will know these deeds, too.

Application

Do everything in the light. Do everything as if the whole world knew the moment you performed the deed.

Someday you will come before Jesus. Do everything as you would want to have done on that day.

On that day the treasures in the bank, the luxury items, the elegant clothes will be embarrassing. The charitable and thoughtful deeds will be glorious.

CHAPTER 28
A NEW WISDOM (10:28-42)

"Do not fear those who deprive the body of life but cannot destroy the soul." (V-28)

Thought

There are two types of death. All experience physical death. Spiritual death comes when the person gives up hope; turns away from ideals; walks away from a task that is within his power; or seizes an advantage through injustice. People fear physical death. Jesus says to fear only spiritual death.

Application

Your life is fraught with many problems. You often have to choose between evils. Some evils only harm your body. Other evils can ruin your soul. Keep your eyes open. Choose physical inconvenience over spiritual death.

"Yet not a single sparrow falls to the ground without your Father's consent." (V-29)

Thought

Notice that the Father doesn't save the sparrows from falling. The curse of death now afflicts the whole planet earth. But nothing happens to them without His consent. They fall to the ground because they have fulfilled their task of glorifying Him by their songs and their joy.

Application
You, unlike the sparrow, experience two kinds of evil. Some evil occurs with the Father's consent. Other evil you bring on yourself by your own free will. He doesn't consent to that. He doesn't intend that evil. If you just trusted the Father like the sparrows do, you would be saved much grief.

"As for you, every hair of your head has been counted; so do not be afraid of anything." (V-30)

Thought
People grow anxious when no one else seems to care about their problems. When another comes, more intelligent and more powerful, they can relax. It's in other hands now.

Application
Jesus says clearly "do not be afraid of anything." Get out some paper, write down everything you fear. By doing this, get the fears outside of yourself. Look at them. They somehow lose their power when seen in the light. Now present them in prayer to the heavenly Father.

"Whoever acknowledges me before men I will acknowledge before my Father in heaven." (V-32)

Thought
What does it mean "to acknowledge Jesus before men?" First, the person has to accept Jesus' authority over himself. Then he acts differently. He listens to the gospel. His thoughts and actions show the

Kingdom of heaven. If asked, he gladly shares the central message of his life, that the Kingdom is at hand.

Application
Do you fulfill these three steps? Do you accept Jesus' authority over you? Do you live according to the gospel? Are you willing to openly acknowledge what is within? Or do you keep your light under a bushel basket?

"My mission is to spread, not peace, but division." (V-34)

Thought
How could Jesus say "Peace I leave you" and then say His mission is not to spread peace? The peace He promises is within, a sense of being right with God? The war he predicts is outside the person.

The war He prepares people for is with the world. Others won't accept Jesus' values, nor even leave in peace those who do.

Application
Don't accept "peace at any price." Sometimes the price is too high. When the price is the giving up of Jesus' Kingdom and the renunciation of the gospels' teaching, then you should choose division over peace.

"In short, to make a man's enemies those of his own household." (V-36)

Thought
Jesus is not naive about the ingrained power of sin. His message strikes at the heart. He sees the clutches of sin. He has no illusion about its power or its reaction or its hold upon every person. When a person accepts His

message, the first to know are the members of his own household. They will be the first to react.

Application
You will have your first moment of truth when you are challenged by those close to you. Then you will see how much you prize your gift of Jesus. Will you allow your friends to take God's word away from you, as the birds stole the seed? Or, will the word truly have gone deeply within you. If so, nothing can uproot it, not even a challenge from your own household.

"he who will not take up his cross and come after me is not worthy of me." (V-38)

Thought
Jesus knows what spiritual warfare involves. He has already been through the temptations. He faces daily the warfare from the Scribes and Pharisees. He doesn't seek followers who just flow with the current stream of thought. His disciples must follow in Jesus' stream, no matter how the world's current is flowing.

Application
Don't get upset by difficulties. You have a work to do. Certain problems have to be faced. Don't cop out on Jesus. Your greatest gift is to be worthy of him.

CHAPTER 29
ELIJAH HAS COME (11:1-15)

"Are you, `he who is to come'
or do we look for an other?" (V-3)

Thought

With 2000 years of hind sight, we see clearly that Jesus is "He who is to come." At least, we see clearly in theory. Practice is something different. We often "look for another." We don't see Jesus as our "All." The present need or future anxiety pulls us away. We look in another direction.

Application

Don't be afraid to ask. Faith doesn't automatically supply all the answers. Let your questions be sincere, flowing from your inner searching. Be a person who seeks the truth and wants to know God's will.

"Go look and report to John what
you hear and see..." (V-4)

Thought

The miracles show the Kingdom is at hand. John preached the same message. However, multiple and clear signs didn't accompany his work. In Jesus, the Kingdom's power increases. The signs multiply and even the doubters have to believe.

Application

You should see the Kingdom manifested every day by God's power. You should see little signs of God's love and little wonders of His protection. Your food and clothing and housing should be signs. The many problems that get solved are His wonders. In seeing these, you begin to see Jesus' Kingdom.

"Blest is the man who finds no stumbling block in me." (V-6)

Thought

The list of wonders includes the blind, lame, deaf, cripple and even the dead being raised to life. How could anyone not believe? Yet, we know the story. Many who saw these miracles did find Jesus a "stumbling block." Miracles and wondrous signs didn't beget faith. Many saw and didn't believe.

Application

Don't underestimate your faith. Rejoice that Jesus is not your stumbling block. Rejoice that you believe. Don't be gloomy as if you have little faith. You believe in Jesus and in the Kingdom. Begin there. What seems little to you is really a great gift from God.

"What did you go out to the wasteland to see..." (V-7)

Thought

Jesus' questions always pierce. Just why did they run out to the desert? Probably every person had a different reason. Some went to see a celebrity. Others, to stare at a holy man or to challenge or to seek God's grace or to listen to his message.

The bigger question is "When they got there, what did they see?" Jesus never blamed anyone for running out into the desert. He did ask that permanent changes result.

Application

When you seek God, you have various reasons. Don't wait for the perfect reason. Whatever gets you to seek Him is good enough. When you go out to the desert,

95

allow yourself to be changed. When you find Jesus, surrender your life.

"I send my messenger ahead of you to prepare your way before you." (V-10)

Thought

John was great. No greater man was born of woman. But he was only a messenger. If so, then who is this Jesus?

We know the right answers. He is God. He is the Word made flesh. He is the Lord and Savior. Are those answers just words or do we really understand.

Application

God has sent you many messengers. Many times He has said to you, that the Lord is coming. This very book is His messenger. Whatever opens your eyes and your ears are messengers to you. The King is coming! Today He comes! This hour He comes! Be ready.

"I solemnly assure you, history has not known a man born of woman greater then John the Baptizer. Yet the least born into the Kingdom of God is greater than he." (V-11)

Thought

The least in the Kingdom is greater than John because Jesus has come. In Jesus, we are children of the Faith, temples of the Spirit, members of the Kingdom. In Jesus we live and move and are. We are new creatures. "Dearly beloved, we are God's children now; what we shall later be has not yet come to light." (1 Jn 3:2)

96

Application

You are all these things right now. You don't become these when you die and go to heaven. The Spirit already has been given to you. You who are the least in the Kingdom are greater than John the Baptizer. John could only say that the Kingdom is at hand. For you, the Kingdom has come.

"If you are prepared to accept it, he is Elijah, the one who was certain to come." (V-14)

Thought

Elijah was to be the last sign before the Messiah. The Jews read the Old Testament literally. They thought that Elijah had to come physically back to earth. They didn't realize that the prophecy would be fulfilled in someone like John who preached in the power of Elijah.

By these words Jesus teaches clearly that the final prophecy had been fulfilled. The Messiah could come at any moment.

Application

Strip away any preconceived obstacles to God's work. Saying "Elijah hasn't yet come" was an excuse for not accepting Jesus.

Don't use any excuses. Don't say you are too young or too old; or not worthy or not ready. The Kingdom can't wait. Jesus comes now. There is no way you can prepare. He comes unexpectedly as the Gift of the Father. Surrender to Him and rejoice.

CHAPTER 30
FAILURE TO REFORM (11:16-24)

"What comparison can I use to describe this breed?" (V-16)

Thought

Jesus grows impatient with the non-responding Jews. He reached for a symbol to describe their attitude. They are like a brick wall, offering nothing but deafness to the message. They use excuses "to listen but not to hear."

Application

Don't judge God's word. Let God's word judge you. Stand under His word, using it as a lamp for your steps.

Don't ask God to speak often. Follow Him the first time He speaks. Be generous and quick to respond.

They are like children squatting in the town squares, calling to their playmates..." (V-16)

Thought

Jesus reduces the learned scribes and Pharisees to the town's playing children. The example is children at their worst. They are selfish, stubborn, going along with no one's suggestions.

Application

Are you willing to see yourself as you really are? As others see you? You will be saved from selfishness only by truth. Accept your own failings, your own shortcomings, and your own sins. Accepting truth about yourself is the wonderful tonic that removes illusions.

"We piped you a tune but you did not dance! We sang you a dirge but you did not wail!" (V-17)

Thought

Jesus finds His comparison in this saying. He wants no one to miss the point, so He interprets it for everyone. John led an ascetical life. He was separated and set a part from others. Jesus led a very ordinary life. He lived in the middle of the people. Both preached the same message. Yet neither was

believed. The Jews were like children who didn't like to hear a joyful song or a dirge.

Application

What do you need to hear God's word? Do you need times of material abundance? Yet, do you not forget God in your good fortune? Do you need times of trial? Yet, do you not question God for permitting difficulties? For you is there never the right time nor the right means to hear God's word? Really, every time, good or bad, should be the moment to hear God.

"Yet time will prove where wisdom lies." (V-19)

Thought

Time has shown that Jesus is the very center of all time. What about the Scribes and Pharisees? We don't even know their names. They are known only for their opposition and hard-heartedness.

Application

Walk in wisdom today. Choose what will last and perdure. Listen to the Spirit of Jesus within. He will store up for you treasure that does not perish. Don't wait for time to show you where wisdom lies. Wisdom lies in Jesus. Listen to His words

99

He began to reproach the towns where most of his miracles had been worked, with their failure to reform. (V-20)

Thought

People like to experience miracles. It shows God's special love and that the reign of God is at hand. People shouldn't just walk away from a miracle. They should reform their lives. Miracles come from God as invitations to reform.

Application

What in your life needs to be reformed? Take out some paper. List those parts clearly. Don't hide them, especially from yourself. Face them clearly. God will do even greater works in you once you have reformed.

"...If the miracles worked in you had taken place in Tyre and Sidon, they would have reformed in sackcloth and ashes long ago." (V-21)

Thought

Again, Jesus reaches for a comparison. He seeks examples of *depravity, - Tyre and Sidon. He then credits them with full reform* and penance. A sharper image couldn't be found.

Application

Everyday, you can receive the Eucharist. You rightly rejoice in the gift. But what can be expected from you? Not even the impenitent towns of Chorazin and Bethsaida had that miracle. The daily Eucharist calls you to reform.

"As for you, Capernaum, Are you to be exalted to the skies? You shall go down to the realm of death?" (V-23)

100

Thought

The gospel always speaks of large crowds following Jesus. His laments over the impenitent towns show that only a few people became true disciples. For the rest, the miracles were just surface words bringing no real commitment to Jesus.

Application

Has the gospel ever reached your core? Have you surrendered your life to Jesus?

No other way exists. You can't give part of your life to the Kingdom. Jesus wants everything. Anything else is not reform. It is just whitewash, not commitment, just flirtation, not surrender. Just dilly-dallying, not seeking the Kingdom.

CHAPTER 31
REVEALING TO THE LITTLE ONES
(11:25-30)

**On one occasion Jesus spoke thus:
"Father, Lord of heaven and earth,
to you I offer praise;..." (V-25)**

Thought

Jesus put everything in right order. He wanted first the Father's glory. He sought everything else for the Father's glory. Jesus was alive to the Father. Whether in prayer or with the crowds, He was always present to the Father. "The Son cannot do anything by Himself - He can do only what He sees the Father doing." (Jn. 5:19)

Application

Jesus wants to share His life with the Father. This sharing is real, beginning in your Baptism. Your life is like a bottle. If it is already filled with selfish pursuits, then Jesus can't give you the Father's life. First, you must be emptied to receive the gift.

"what you have hidden from the learned and the clever you have revealed to the merest children." (V-25)

Thought

Jesus enjoys the contrast. These hidden mysteries bypass the clever and learned. The gift is opened wide to the disciples.

Jesus understood the Father's mysteries. Like any preacher, He did everything to prepare the disciples' minds. However, the full gift came through their own personal enlightenment.

Application

You cannot earn faith. The gift comes down from the Father of Lights. Just as the virgins couldn't hurry the bridegroom's coming, you cannot hurry this gift. You can search and ask and want. You can seek and not grow discouraged. When you least expect, the Father will bestow the gift.

"You have graciously willed it so." (V-26)

Thought

As a doctor understands the world of medicine, Jesus understood the Kingdom. Everywhere He saw its reality and presence. He knew every person could be changed by its power. He rejoiced that the Apostles were beginning to see. Jesus now had companions in the Kingdom, like a first-born son with his younger brothers and sisters.

Application

The Father wants you in His Kingdom. He made you for His Kingdom. Jesus wants you as His brother and sister. Your life, mortal and immortal, depends on your receiving the Kingdom. The Father wills it so. Let the Kingdom come!

"...no one knows the Father but the Son - and anyone to whom the Son wishes to reveal him." (V-27)

Thought

This stress on personal enlightenment is the central theme of John's gospel. However, both Matthew and Luke also have the same invitation. Inner enlightenment is not the message of just one gospel. The Kingdom only comes by internal change and reception.

Application

How do you know you have accepted the Kingdom? There must be some inner act of receiving. Do you feel God's power? Do you find yourself thinking of the Father, seeking the Kingdom, wanting His presence? Don't stop with externals. Search until the Son reveals the Father to you.

"Come to me, all you who are weary and find life burdensome." (V-28)

Thought

How does a person "come" to Jesus? During His mortal life, that was easy. The crowds learned to find Him. But now that he has "been taken up," how does a person come to Jesus? Magdalene complained "They have taken Him away." Nicodemus asked "How can this happen?"

We are more fortunate, knowing that the risen body of Jesus is not limited by mortality, nor time nor space.

Application

Don't move. Don't seek Jesus here or there. Don't go to the upper room or out into the desert. Jesus is already with you. He has been there all the time. "Coming to Jesus" means allowing your eyes and ears to be opened.

"I will refresh you." (V-28)

Thought

We associate "refreshing" with water, either drinking or bathing or cleansing. The Spirit that Jesus gives is "the living water." (Jn. 7:38 and Rev. 22:1). He gives tears, feelings, light, wisdom and peace. The Spirit is the deepest water that man can experience.

Application

Do you experience the Spirit of Jesus? He lives in you through your baptismal waters. His refreshment comes daily. Without these consolations and inner helps, you cannot be refreshed. If you aren't refreshed by Jesus, you will turn to other waters for your consolation.

"Take my yoke upon your shoulders." (V-29)

Thought

Jesus was the carpenter's son. Each animal was fitted for his yoke. The yoke didn't rub or cause undue pain. The carpenter fashioned the yoke just right.

Application

Don't be your own carpenter, fashioning your own yoke. Your yoke will be too small, too large, too wide or too narrow. Be a child of God, see clearly that the yoke Jesus asks you to carry is perfect for you.

CHAPTER 32
EATING AND CURING ON THE SABBATH
(12:1-15)

"See here! Your disciples are doing what is not permitted on the Sabbath." (V-2)

Thought

Who does not permit this? God provided the food. Why are God's purposes thwarted?

Men twist God's message. Therefore, many don't accept this preaching. Jesus understands the Father. When He preaches, all listen.

Application

Don't be deceived by any man-made message. Jesus offers you new freedom. You are nobody's servant except His. The earth is your Father's house. Accept no bonds or shackles. You are God's child. Don't let the world confuse you or destroy God's image within you.

"have you not read what David did when he and his men were hungry..." (V-3)

Thought

Jesus knew the Scriptural stories. He knew how God's servants acted, lived and made decisions. No one could foist upon Jesus a false tradition. He was in contact with the living tradition of those who walked with God.

Application

Do you know the scriptural stories? Do you read the lives of the saints? Do you know the Church's teachings? They are God's living word. Be formed in those traditions and no one will deceive you.

"I assure you there is something greater than the temple here." (V-6)

Thought
The Pharisees started this argument. They thought they had a clear law.

Jesus brings in David, the holy bread and the priest on temple duty. He doesn't let the Pharisees center upon secondary questions, like pulling off the heads of grain.

Application
Don't be preoccupied with secondary questions. The important truths concern Jesus and your relationship to Him.

He is greater than the temple. You can leave a temple but you can't get away from Jesus. Accept the mystery. You were made for Jesus!

"...It is mercy I desire and not sacrifice,"...(V-7)

Thought
As people approach Jesus, they experience more freedom. They rejoice at being near someone who loves and understands them. They know they fail. They also know that Jesus desires mercy.

Application
Accept God's mercy. Don't pull away from Jesus because of personal sins or past failures. If you do that regularly, you will never understand the mercy Jesus intends for you.

A man with a shriveled hand happened to be there. (V-10)

Thought

The gospel says "happened," as if everything were accidental. Really nothing just "happens" with God. All is thought out, foreseen and pre-arranged. The only thing that "happens" is our free will when we upset all that God has arranged. Then God rearranges everything. He never lets us get away.

Application

Look on the many "happenings" of your life. You have had parents, teachers, opportunities, decisions, and other people. God arranged everything.

Today, He arranges events. He arranges for you to read this book. He inspires you within. He provides opportunities. Nothing just happens to you. God arranges everything.

"Is it lawful to work a cure on the Sabbath?" (V-10)

Thought

The cure usually given was to provide needed assistance. Jesus' cure will be quite different and a direct sign of His goodness. The whole story points out the folly of postponing good. Why make someone wait for God's favor?

Application

God's time is always "now." Not necessarily for what we want but for what God wants. He never postpones the good. Time is too short. Tomorrow another good is needed. Today is the time for today's gift.

...and it was perfectly restored; it became as sound as the other. (V-13)

Thought

Done perfectly in an instant! Nature is healed by grace. In the gospels we never find Jesus restoring lost hands or feet. Although shriveled, Jesus used the person's hand as it yielded to His power.

Application

What part of you is shriveled? Your feelings, your hopes, your dreams? Possibly, you feel your talent and intellect are shriveled. You keep them hidden from view. Don't do that. Show what is shriveled to Jesus and yield to His power.

CHAPTER 33
THE GENTLE VICTOR (12:16-21)

...he sternly ordered them not to make public what he had done. (V-16)

Thought

Keeping things hidden was prudent. Otherwise Jesus would have to leave the vicinity. If the people let Him work quietly, He could continue among them. Jesus isn't interested in notoriety. He wants solid works hidden from men's eyes.

Application

Keep still about Jesus' work within you. Speaking too freely can ruin the work.

Don't be interested in show or religious respect. Jesus' work in you is too deep for that.

Don't be mixing God's service and man's applause. Live in single-mindedness.

108

"here is my servant whom
I have chosen" (V-18)

Thought

From an exhortation to be quiet, Matthew moves to a public proclamation of Jesus' Messiahship. In Jesus is a unique mystery of the Father.

God has chosen others, but these always point to Jesus. He chose others later, but always in Jesus. There is really only one Chosen of God. The rest of us just share in that choice.

Application

Don't go running around in search of God. Don't pick up books or run off to retreats. Seek Jesus. Only One has been chosen. The rest just share His riches.

"I will endow him with my Spirit..." (V-18)

Thought

The Spirit is an inner gift. He is the deepest given and the deepest received. Both giving and receiving are total. The Spirit demands total emptying out to prepare for a total receiving.

Application

Don't be partial with God. The spirit totally possessed Jesus. Jesus totally yielded to the Spirit. Let go. Surrender everything so you can totally receive.

"he will not contend or cry out..." (V-19)

Thought

Strength sometimes speaks out. It condemns unjust practices. Jesus spoke out but never for Himself. When the time came for Him to suffer, His voice could not be heard in the street.

Being possessed by God's Spirit has its trying moments. The natural reaction would be a complaint. But the words would ruin everything. The gift of sacrifice is completed by the silence.

Application
Don't ruin God's work by complaining. Otherwise, your suffering isn't sanctifying just annoying. Few are really interested in your complaints, no matter how justified. When they hear no complaints, they know the Spirit is acting in you.

"The bruised reed he will not crush,..." (V-20)

Thought
This verse shows the gentleness of Jesus. The bruised reed is helpless, almost waiting to be crushed. The smoldering wick seems ready to be quenched. They represent the helpless people whose rights can easily be usurped. They have no power to resist. Jesus won't take advantage of anyone's helplessness.

Application
How do you treat the powerless and those who are beneath you? How do you act toward your children, your employees, and your subordinates? Do you manipulate, grabbing whatever you can? Or does helplessness call forth care and protection from you?

"...until judgment is made victorious." (V-20)

Thought
Jesus is no loser. Only for a time does He suffer, stay quiet and endure death. After that, His life is filled with authority, power and victory. He is not the eternal "gentle person." Only for a while do the powers of darkness seem to conquer.

Application

Jesus doesn't ask you to lose on purpose. He asks you to put aside your ways. They can win only short-term victories. He shows you a new way. His way guarantees total, final and complete victory.

"In his name, the Gentiles will find hope." (V-21)

Thought

Many thought the Messiah was only for the Jews. The full mystery was revealed slowly. St. Paul understood "That mystery hidden from ages and generations past, but now revealed to his holy ones." (Col. 1:26). Obviously, God's work went far beyond the original boundaries.

Application

You have hopes and desires for your life. In Jesus, even your greatest hopes are small. God's plan for you goes far beyond your ideas. Don't limit God. Don't do things your way. Trust until you are vindicated. Jesus shares His mystery with you.

CHAPTER 34
THE STRONG MAN (12:22-30)

...he cured the man so that he could speak and see. (V-22)

Thought

Jesus came to bring life. Much life is already placed in human nature by the Father. Sin binds and ties that life. People have to lock their doors and stay inside. Fear dominates many a neighborhood. Violence and graft appear wherever large sums of money loom. Our Heavenly Father intended quite a different human life than we daily experience.

111

Application

What "possesses" your life, binding you so you do not freely speak or fully live? Some "blinds" are external. They result from situations. Others are within. They come from your personality and background. Jesus always frees. He has already made you a "new creation." However, your baptismal gift must come forth by your living Jesus' words.

All in the crowd were astonished. (V-23)

Thought

The new freedom always astonishes. We think people will always be the way they were yesterday. We expect the same patterns, the same rut, and the same problems.

Application

Have you ever seen someone set free? It should have had two results, your believing in God's power and your wanting to be free. But what happened? Did your faith pass? With that passing, did you lose the hope that life could be different? Well, accept again the gospel power of Jesus. Believe that His power can change your life.

"Might this not be David's son?" (V-23)
"This man can expel demons only with the help of Beelzebub, the prince of demons." (V-24)

Thought

Two very different reactions. The first is a question. The crowds didn't really know. At least they are open to the possibility of Jesus having David's power.

The second reaction is a definite statement. It's a stupid statement. The Pharisees didn't want to ask the question of the source of Jesus' power.

112

Application

You do the same thing all the time. God speaks and acts. You turn foolishly away. Grace should get you to stop. At least ask the questions. "Is God calling me? Is God acting upon me now?" You won't always respond, but your pause to ask opens you to God.

"A town or household split into factions cannot last for long." (V-25)

Thought

Jesus points out a contradiction that's obvious. Only a fool tolerates a divided household. A split inevitably widens and deepens. Everything collapses.

Application

Don't be a fool. Look at your own house and its divisions. Part of you is for Jesus. Part is for yourself. Another part is with the world. Another part is owned by fear. You are divided. Only Jesus can put you together. So choose Him now as your Lord, your only Lord, and be rid of the divisions.

"But if it is by the Spirit of God that I expel demons, then the reign of God has overtaken you." (V-28)

Thought

Jesus answers the crowd's question. The reign of God has come. Many shook their heads in disbelief. Many said that He went too far in His claims. Jesus' teaching was clear. He was using the full power of His father.

Application

Let the reign of God overtake you. For so long now, you've been searching - often in the wrong way or in the wrong places for the wrong reasons. You don't have to move. You don't have to go anywhere. Read

113

the gospel's words. *The reign of God has overtaken you. Surrender!*

"How can anyone enter a strong man's house..." (V-29)

Thought

Jesus is the strong man. All power in heaven and earth has been given Him. No harm comes to anyone protected by Jesus. He holds on to whomever the Father has given Him.

Application

Look at your children and your house. What would you do if someone broke in and tried to harm them? You would risk your life, even lay down your life, for them. Jesus has done that for you. He does nothing in vain. He is your strong man guarding your treasures. Place your life and your house under His Lordship.

"He who is not with me is against me..." (V-30)

Thought

A deliberate choice is involved here. Jesus doesn't talk about a wish or a hope, or a faint desire. He wants a firm decision of the will. That decision must be full. Everything must be included. Jesus demands all. That might sound extreme, but whatever is not given to Him, He cannot guard.

Application

When you hold back, you lose. When you cling to something, you don't keep it. Foolishness is in saving your life. Wisdom is in giving it away to Jesus.

CHAPTER 35
INNER TRUTH (12:31-42)

"...blasphemy against the Spirit will not be forgiven." (V-31)

Thought

Many good people worry about this text. They wonder if somehow they have committed the unforgivable sin of "blasphemy against the Spirit." They don't realize that Jesus isn't creating a new sin.

Jesus teaches that forgiveness of sins comes from the Spirit (Jn. 20:22-23). If someone denies there is a Spirit, he closes the door to forgiveness.

Application

Don't be confused by this text. You believe in the Spirit. He always will offer you forgiveness. He wants to remove your sins. That is His purpose in coming. Jesus sent Him to forgive.

"...for you can tell a tree by its fruit." (V-33)

Thought

Doctrines about God abound. Some say this. Others preach that. Who can tell anyway? Many don't even want to know. The very confusion delights them. They feel free to pick and choose. Yet results follow beliefs. Confusion breeds the darkness where sin abounds. Truth begets light where Jesus dwells.

Application

Look at the confusing areas of your life. Examine the darkness you experience. Look for means to dispel that darkness. Pray for someone to seek out and ask. Confusion recedes slowly. The ground of truth is made firm little by little.

115

"how can you utter anything good, you brood of vipers, when you are so evil?" (V-34)

Thought

People try to solve problems on the surface. Jesus never allows that to happen. Words come quickly. Jesus never settles for words. If the heart is evil, no matter what the words sound like, they are not good.

Application

Jesus won't let you get away with just a new outside appearance. He started His baptismal work in you with the Holy Spirit's presence. He expects you to be "good to the core." He wants no sham. No cover-up. He wants goodness within and without.

"A good man produces good from his store of goodness." (V-35)

Thought

A person cannot draw out what they have never placed in the storeroom. Life isn't magic. What the man has stored up over the years is himself. He is whatever he has placed in his heart. Jesus always said what a person put on their tongue wasn't really important. What they allowed into their heart determined everything.

Application

You are free. You are not determined by the past, or your background, or your personality. You can choose what to put into your heart. But don't start tomorrow. The choice is now. You will be tomorrow what you put in your heart today.

"By your words you will be acquitted, and by your words you will be condemned." (V-37)

Thought
Words create an atmosphere. There are words of tension, confrontation and anger. There are also words of acceptance, oneness and peace. Words flow freely. They are often unguarded and thoughtless. There are selfish words, manipulative words, hurting and crushing words. Other words come from the Spirit. These overcome sin and destroy evil.

Application
What words do you speak? Don't bother counting your words or measuring your words. That is too shallow. Ask how you feel? How you think? What goes on in your heart? They are the words you are speaking. No wonder you will be acquitted or condemned by them.

"An evil and unfaithful age is eager for a sign!" (V-39)

Thought
A sign is external. It is easily shrugged off or dismissed. Signs never change hearts. For those who believe, no sign is necessary. For those who don't believe, no sign is enough.

Application
Are you faithful to God when no signs are given? Are you His before He does wonders for you? Are you His in illness, disgrace, collapse or rejection? Are you His in good times and in difficult times? The times don't matter. Being His certainly does.

"...so will the Son of Man spend three days and three nights in the bowels of the earth." (V-40)

Thought
Once the Resurrection occurred, human history was never the same. New power had come. A sign had

been given. The visions touched the hearts of the disciples. And their message went out to all the world. He is risen!

Application
You who were baptized have also risen. You were submerged with Jesus in your Baptismal water. You have come up with Him. Your life is already with God. You haven't just been given the sign. You have experienced the sign. If the bowels of the earth could not hold Jesus, then no power can hold you who have been baptized in Jesus.

CHAPTER 36
RESISTING OUTSIDE INFLUENCES
(12:43-50)

"...it roams through arid wastes..." (V-43)

Thought
The mountaintop is symbolic of man talking to God. The desert is the symbolic place for evil spirits. In the desert, a person is alone and open to fears. In the desert food and drink are not available. In the desert the regular provisions given to mankind by the Heavenly Father are missing.

Application
As you eat and drink of the Body and Blood of Jesus, you are kept free from the evil one. The Eucharist is your food for your journey. No need for you to dwell in arid places.

"I will go back where I came from..." (V-44)

118

Thought

Tendencies come back. Old habits continue to haunt. Memories, addictions, past sins retain their power.

Application

Only Jesus can set you free. Freedom comes through the blood of Jesus.

You do not wash once and hope to remain clean the rest of your life. Washing is a daily task. Being washed with the blood of Jesus is also a daily gift.

"...returns to find the dwelling unoccupied, though swept and tidied now." (V-44)

Thought

This famous line symbolizes the lazy person who has experienced Jesus' freedom from evil. However, he has done absolutely nothing since. Being free, the person can choose and decide. He now has his own thoughts and desires. He is no longer obsessed. However, he does nothing positive and becomes prone to the former obsession.

Application

When Jesus frees you, you should rejoice always (Phil. 4:4). You also have to use your freedom. Find others to serve. Grow closer to your family. Use your freedom or it will be taken away from you, like the buried talents.

"They move in and settle there." (V-45)

Thought

How did they get back in? The door was left open. The tree was uprooted, but nothing filled in the holes. The task wasn't completed. The addictions were taken away but the occasions of sin weren't removed. The person was lifted from the pit, but continued to walk around the edge. Evil has an unmistakable fascination. Just allowing its presence, gives power to evil.

Application

Look at your addictions. These are evils that claim you and have power over you. Freedom must come from outside, through the delivering power of Jesus. Once free, you must do your part. Put the evil at a distance. Fill in any openings in your personality that would permit re-entry.

His mother and his brothers, appeared outside to speak to him. (V-46)

Thought

They came out of kindness. They were worried about Him and the reactions coming from others. They heard the threats. They knew the gossip. However, Jesus knew His course.

Application

When people come to you, listen. They frequently come in kindness. Their words might be God's guidance for you. Sometimes, however, their words are to be set aside. You should stay on your course.

"Who is my mother? Who are my brothers?" (V-48)

Thought

Jesus had to raise this question because sometimes family members resist the Father's will. The ideal is when physical mothers and brothers are also spiritual mothers and brothers. But this isn't always true.

Application

When you find Jesus, think first of your family members. Your life is interwoven with them. You need their support in this new life. You should want to share this life with them. However, if they oppose the Kingdom of God, you cannot just give up this gift for their sake.

"Whoever does the will of my heavenly father is brother and sister and mother to me." (V-50)

Thought

It is a wonderful gift to have parents and brothers and sisters. They are primary relationships, the foundation of emotional life. Deprivation in the family causes a lifelong scar.

But Jesus brings a new mystery. In Him, we are all /brothers and sisters sharing the same Baptismal life. Yet this truth doesn't have much effect. People, even the baptized, don't understand all the Kingdom's gifts.

Application

Let yourself be brother and sister to all of God's household. You know how you act toward your own brothers and sisters. You forgive, overlook mistakes, and lend support. Act the same with others. Jesus wants to provide many parents, brothers and sisters for you.

CHAPTER 37
SOWING THE WORD (13:1-9; 18-23)

"Part of it fell on rocky ground." (V-5)

Thought

No soil here, only hardness of heart. Nothing for the seed to be rooted into, no receptivity. This ground won't yield at all. Jesus always looked for openness. He wanted people willing to change.

Application

Do you think you know exactly what you want? Do you think you have everything together? Then, you probably have no receptivity. You probably feel that you don't need God's seed.

"...part of the seed fell among thorns..." (V-7)

Thought

The farmer seems a little careless. He tossed the seed on thorns. He should scatter the seed on ground where it could possibly grow to harvest. Maybe he feels that he has lots of seeds. He doesn't mind losing some.

Application

Do you throw away time, opportunities, moments of grace? Do you throw away days, feeling you have plenty of time? Soon your bag will be empty and there will be no harvest.

"Part of it, finally, landed on good soil." (V-8)

Thought

It seemed such a long wait. Maybe only a handful of seed was still left. All is not lost. The return is a thirty, sixty and hundred to one.

Application

You might see your life as wasted. Look into your bag again. Isn't there at least a handful of seed still remaining? Nothing is lost yet. Look for the good ground of eternal life.

"The seed along the path is the man who hears the message about God's reign without understanding it." (V-19)

Thought

God's word is a teaching. When people hear those words they use their intellects. A teaching has to be pondered, pursued, thought out and applied (as we try to do here). If not, people don't see it's importance, and allow even the birds to steal it.

Application

What do you think about each day? You certainly use your thinking to make a living. You should turn it also to God's word and store up eternal treasures.

"The seed that fell on patches of rock is the man who hears the message and at first receives it with joy. But he has no roots, so he lasts only for a time." (V-20-21)

Thought

A person needs roots. A person needs a family, a neighborhood, a job, and friends. These save from discouragement, isolation, loneliness and a hundred other ills. These roots depend on the person's decision. A person joins with others or decides to be a loner.

Application

Don't retreat into your lonely world. Don't isolate yourself. Maintain your family relationships. Don't go off on your own. Others are important to you. If uprooted, you will succumb.

123

"What was sown among briers is the man who hears the message, but then worldly anxiety and the lure of money choke it off." (V-22)

Thought

This condition is called "the unsettled heart." People feel the grass is greener elsewhere. Supposedly they are missing out on something. They give up what they have, toss it all aside, and leave behind what they have pursued for years.

Application

You have to face some attractions within you. Otherwise, they will ruin everything. Everyone has them. You are no different. You can be swept away by the excitement of new possibilities. You can fantasize about a better life. You have worked hard at something. It is truly worthwhile. Be patient and don't be lured away.

"But what was sown on good soil is the man who hears the message and takes it in." (V-23)

Thought

A person chooses what is valuable. The person abandons what is worthless. Everyone has that choice about God's word. The person takes it in or leaves it outside. The decision depends on how important the person sees God's word.

Application

Nothing in your life is as valuable as God's word. To lay down your life for God's word or to build your house upon God's word is the work of a wise man. Cherish the word. Take it in deeply. The fruit is eternal life with Jesus.

124

CHAPTER 38
UNDERSTANDING PARABLES
(13:10-17; 31-35)

"Why do you speak to them in parables?" (V-10)

Thought

That is a good question. If Jesus is the light of the world, why doesn't He speak openly rather than in parables.

Because religious truth is not mathematical truth. The gospel doesn't force itself upon anyone. The preached message is an invitation waiting for the person's response.

Application

Don't approach the gospels with a testing mind, one that always needs proof. God doesn't convince you of truths. He invites you to life. The gospel should enlighten you about the decisions you make this day. You should see clearly the world moving in one direction and the Kingdom calling you to a different response.

"To you has been given a knowledge of the mysteries of the reign of God..." (V-11)

Thought

What a beautiful definition of faith. It is not just assent to truths; not just knowledge; not just even hidden mysteries. Faith moves the person into the kingdom. Without this "knowledge of the mysteries," the person stands outside. He never enjoys the wisdom of the little ones.

Application
What have you done with this "knowledge of the mysteries?" Do you put it on a shelf, taking it down for your Sunday Church attendance? Do you bury this knowledge in the ground? Or does this knowledge live inside you? Does it light your way and lead you to decisions? Is the reign of God alive in you or has its power long ago died?

"To the man who has, more will be given until he grows rich; the man who has not, will lose what little he has." (V-12)

Thought
This seems grossly unfair, but God's Spirit is given to multiply the Father's riches in us. That's the normal process. A person should grow rich in the Kingdom. If that's not happening then why let the lazy, unproductive person continue to have the Spirit.

Application
You never see yourself as rich in the Kingdom. For you, the Kingdom seems so far away. But the Spirit is within. Every hope, every prayer, every cup of cold water multiplies His gifts. Grow in the Kingdom. Multiplying God's gifts is the normal process.

"Listen as you will, you shall not understand, look intently as you will, you shall not see." (V-14)

Thought
This saying, although seemingly unfair, highlights the stubbornness of the Pharisees. They are spiritually dead and blind. Their hearts won't open to the truth.

Application
Don't substitute religious activity for surrendering. Don't say endless prayers or read every spiritual book.

126

First, give your heart to God. Then your prayers and reading will have results.

"but blest are your eyes because they see and blest are your ears because they hear." (V-16)

Thought

For most people, faith in Jesus comes from family and neighborhood Church. The teaching was there from the beginning. The person was taught about God, Jesus' coming, and the Eucharist.

These gifts are so great and so present from life's beginning that every person has to reflect to appreciate.

Application

Just because you didn't work for your faith, doesn't lessen the gift. Because God through your parents and your parish gave you the faith only increases the gift. A gift is a gift. Trying to pay for a gift is foolish. Only thanksgiving and appreciation are required.

"The reign of God is like a mustard seed which someone took and sowed in this field." (V-31)

Thought

The person didn't see these seeds as important. Since they were available the man threw them into his field. He probably forgot for the longest while that the event ever happened.

Application

One day an invitation arrived that didn't seem too important. Yet, you accepted and went. Your life was changed. You realize now that the invitation was like the mustard seed. You didn't know all that God had in store for you.

"...yet when full-grown it is the largest of plants." (V-32)

Thought

God's gifts are small at first but they never stop growing. That's the two-fold mystery. Without faith, the person overlooks the little seeds. He chooses bigger gifts that really have no life.

God's seeds never stop within the person. They always produce change until the person is safely in the Kingdom.

Application

How do you choose God's little seeds? It is easy. Cleanse your heart of ambition, selfishness and anxiety. Stop chasing after people with big reputations who supposedly can get you something. Then be still. You will see that each day contains God's seeds.

CHAPTER 39
WHEAT AND WEEDS (13:24-30; 36-43)

"...a man who sowed good seed in his field." (V-24)
"...his enemy came and sowed weeds..." (V-25)

Thought

The field is the person's inner self, containing both the Holy Spirit and the powers of original sin. Within each person is the greatest courage or the grossest ambition. Both are there. Every possible good and evil is sown within everyone.

Application

Don't pretend. You are no different. You are not all evil. God has placed good seeds there. You are not all good. The enemy has also done his work. You face a basic question. What seeds do you yield to?

128

"...the weeds made their appearance as well."
(V-26)

Thought

That appearance can be overwhelming. The person grows disheartened. He doesn't understand. Suddenly the powers of evil seem everywhere and in complete control.

Application

Don't be surprised. Anything can happen to you. However, nothing is final until the end. The appearance of weeds isn't the final story. The wheat is growing too. Be faithful until the harvest.

"Where are the weeds coming from?" (V-27)

Thought

The servants thought the world was simple. Wheat was planted. Only wheat should grow. That is not life. Complications set in. Gaining the Kingdom isn't as simple as it seemed at first. Unforeseen obstacles start appearing.

Application

Don't be discouraged. The parable has a happy ending. It is meant to encourage you. Obstacles shouldn't cause you to give up. Don't complain that you didn't foresee all these problems. Stay with the task. You will be shown a solution.

"Do you want us to go out and pull them up?
" (V-28)

Thought

The servants aren't discouraged, but they aren't heading in the right direction either. They don't weigh the consequences. They would act impulsively and without wisdom.

Application
Wanting to do good isn't enough. You need wisdom. Otherwise you will be acting foolishly. You will have few results and will ruin God's work.

"Let them grow together until harvest..." (V-30)

Thought
The owner never took his eyes off the goal. He didn't want a beautiful, weedless field. He wanted a wheat harvest. His solution didn't ruin but preserved the wheat. That is wisdom.

Application
What is your goal? What do you want in a given situation? To look good? To feel justified? To win the argument? Or do you want reconciliation, peace and forgiveness? If you really want the right goals, God will show you His solutions.

"The farmer sowing good seed is the Son of Man;" (V-37) "...the field is the world, the good seed the citizens of the kingdom." (V-38)

Thought
That is the ideal picture of the Church. Wherever Jesus has sent His Spirit, all are "citizens of the Kingdom." Unfortunately, it is not true. The real picture is a field mixed with wheat and weeds.

Application
You have little control over others. They make their own choices. For your part, stay faithful to what Jesus has sown within you.

"The weeds are the followers of the evil one..." (V-38) "and the enemy who sowed them is the devil." (V-39)

Thought
How did they get mixed in? Shouldn't they have their separate field? But there is no separate field. There is only the one world.

Application
Everyone should belong to the Kingdom. In truth many people are weeds, yielding to the evil sowed within. You have to face that truth. The weeds aren't far away. They grow right next to you and are closely interwoven. That causes problems. The weeds can strangle the wheat. You have no choice. You must grow side by side. Just don't be entangled.

CHAPTER 40
COMING UPON THE KINGDOM
(13:44-58)

"The reign of God is like a buried treasure which a man found in a field." (V-44)

Thought
Jesus doesn't say whether the man was looking for the treasure or just stumbled upon it. At other times, Jesus teaches people to seek and ask. Here, He stresses the "finding," and describes the man's feelings. Sometimes, people say that feelings don't matter in religion. This parable seems to highlight the religious feelings in finding the Kingdom.

Application
What are your feelings about the Kingdom? Have you ever found this treasure? Has there ever been a beginning religious experience? Do you experience God being close to you?

131

"...rejoicing at his find went and sold all he had and bought that field." (V-44)

Thought

Why did the man rejoice? He had found something outside himself, that was valuable enough to surrender all he had. Everyone gives away his life. Most end up giving it away to useless endeavors. That is failure. Joy comes when the person finds something so valuable that it's worth giving away his very life.

Application

Do you rejoice? What do you live for? What can pull you outside yourself and set you free? Have you come upon your life's treasure? When you find the Kingdom, you will truly rejoice.

"...like a merchant's search for find pearls." (V-45)

Thought

Here, Jesus stresses the "search." Finding the Kingdom isn't just a hopeless, stumbling upon. Planned seeking is involved. How does a merchant do this searching, trial and error? Many false hopes and many empty shells. But the searching is daily and regular. It is not half hearted or sporadic.

Application

You need to be consistent in searching for God. Days of fervor, followed by weeks of aimlessness, are not the way. Begin now. Listen to the God within. The search for the Kingdom begins the finding.

"...like a dragnet thrown into the lake, which collected all sorts of things." (V-47)

Thought

The Kingdom isn't limited to one personality type, or one age group, or even one nation or people. The net

132

goes everywhere. It catches "all sorts of things." They come in all sizes and shapes.

Many people don't see themselves as pious or devout. When hearing about the "Reign of God" they feel that the gift just can't be for them.

Application
The "Reign of God" is for you. No matter who you are, your age or background. The net will collect you. Jesus went to all the towns, to homes and to work places. He brought the Kingdom to fishermen, tax-collectors, and women (good and not so good). He wants to bring the Reign to you.

"...sat down to put what was worthwhile into containers." (V-48)

Thought
Who is worthwhile? Who is saved in a container? Whoever holds on to the message. Whoever is changed by the Kingdom. Whoever surrenders to the Reign.

Application
There is only one question. Is Jesus Christ everything to you? Would you lay down your life for Him?

On a more practical note, did you think of Him, today? Did you live as He wanted, today? Were you a child of the world or a child of the Kingdom, today?

"What was useless they threw away." (V-48)

Thought
This theme keeps recurring. What is not of the Kingdom is tossed away. Seems extreme. However, what matters at the end of life? What a person did for others and for God; the moments (and even years) that

he gave away; these are the truly valuable. Everything else, all the selfish moments, are really worthless. Seeing that truth only at death is useless knowledge.

Application
Jesus wants you to see now. The selfish acts of this day are useless. The good deeds will be gathered up and saved.

When you took time with another; when you turned your thoughts to God; when you were patient and charitable, will be gather up in the net and put in God's container.

"...like the head of a household who can bring from his storeroom both the new and the old." (V-52)

Thought
The Kingdom is not simple, because life itself is complicated. The person's heart must be simple, but his mind must be filled with varied wisdom.

Everything placed in a storeroom was put there ahead of time. The person can only pull out what he painstakingly has stored away.

Application
Becoming "learned in the Reign of God" takes time. You can't accomplish it overnight. If you let time go by and don't bother to become "learned in the Kingdom" then you will have nothing to bring forth.

CHAPTER 41
THE TRULY PROVEN KING - JESUS
(14:1-12)

"This man is John the Baptizer - It is he in person, raised from the dead;..." (V-2)

Thought

What a silly statement, and it comes from a king! Herod had a long way to go. He had no religious training.

Others have learned a lot about God or the Church. Yet they feel it hasn't done them too much good. Probably more has been accomplished than they realize. At least they have a foundation, a beginning point. They can reach out to God from there.

Application

You have many doctrines that you learned from childhood. You even have prayers you memorized. Maybe that's all you have.

Well, begin there. Think about the truths. Say the prayers slowly. Use what you have and you will begin to find the Kingdom.

Recall that Herod had had John arrested. (V-3)

Thought

Herod saw himself as powerful. Because of his powers he saw himself as free to do as he pleased. Herod was wrong. He judged in earthly terms. He didn't acknowledge the Kingdom's power.

Application

You can easily see Herod's poor judgment. He should have acknowledged God's power in John. The same question confronts you. You live in the midst of powers. You exercise some and are influenced by others. Do you acknowledge God's power over you? Do you refuse to be intimidated by other powers? Do you see your own powers limited by God's will? Or do you think you can do whatever you want?

Herod wanted to kill John, but was afraid of the people. (V-5)

Thought

Everyone who plays with power, lives in fear. Other people with powers greater than theirs, are always on hand. Look at the powerful of this world. They live in fear because others have more power.

Application

If power is your kingdom, then you will be filled with fear. Fear shows that the reign of God is not yet firmly established within you. Accept the power of Jesus over you. You will never have to worry about some greater power. No one has greater power than Jesus.

Herodias' daughter performed a dance (V-6)

Thought

The powerful king gets tricked by a woman and her daughter. They play upon his secret fears. He is not a free person. He is a king, but he does not even control what is inside himself.

Application

Don't seek freedom and power outside yourself. Outside possessions increase anxieties. True freedom comes from within. Inner strength comes by surrendering to Jesus.

All are weak. All are powerless. Only the children of the Kingdom have been freed from fears.

136

The king immediately had his misgivings. (V-9)

Thought

No one can blot out a memory. No one can really lie to themselves. Guilt is already within, because guilt begins from within. "Misgivings" spread throughout the feelings and control everything.

Application

How do you handle guilt? Many solutions only compound the problem. When you have done wrong, be truthful. Be sorry and seek God's forgiveness. You will be set right. The guilt won't control you.

He sent the order to have John beheaded in prison. (V-10)

Thought

The king really lost his own head. He was swept along by outside powers. He had no inner strength to plot his own course.

He had freely begun, choosing to imprison John. By the end, he was doing everybody's will but his own. Even a king can lose his freedom and power.

Application

Jesus wants you to keep your freedom. He doesn't want you swept away. Every day, many powers exert their pressure on you. You can't keep your freedom just by willing it. You aren't strong enough for that. Freedom comes when your will is rooted in the Spirit sent by Jesus.

Afterward, they came and informed Jesus. (V-12)

Thought

This chapter began with Herod thinking Jesus was the risen John. This verse again links John with Jesus.

What an honor to be so closely connected to Jesus! Jesus Himself said that the least in the Kingdom is connected even more closely to Him than John.

Application

You see Jesus as far away. You consider Him someone who lived 2000 years ago. You see yourself as one of millions. You are no one special. To Jesus, you are special. You're a child in His Kingdom. His Spirit lives in you through Baptism. No one has to inform Jesus of anything that happens to you. He sees everything. He is present to you in every situation.

CHAPTER 42
A PERSONAL DESIRE FOR EUCHARIST
(14:13-21)

The crowds heard of it and followed him on foot from the towns. (V-13)

Thought

The "it" refers to Jesus going off to a desert place. The crowds react immediately to the news. No delays. No putting off until tomorrow. They want to be with Jesus. The Pharisees and Scribes can say and think what they want. No one is going to hold back the crowd. They know that someone special is in their midst.

Application

By Baptism, the Spirit lives within you and moves in the same way. He is the Spirit of Jesus. Through Him you hear about Jesus. He speaks to you. He asks no delay or hesitancy. Soon, you will be responding promptly like the crowds did.

He cured their sick. (V-14)

Thought

Jesus didn't just stand around and offer pity. He brought power. The crowds never doubted. He had never let them down. He gave them teachings, bread, consoling words and healings. Never had he left them disappointed. Their faith in Him was too simple for that.

Application

Sophistication can get in the way. You will receive the Kingdom as a child, or not at all. Jesus will never disappoint you. However, you give up too quickly. You stop asking. Once He gets into His boat, you think you can't get to Him. Learn from the crowd. Discover where He is and seek Him out.

When he disembarked and saw the vast throng, his heart was moved with pity. (V-14)

Thought

No one manipulated the crowd. No advertising campaign whipped them into a frenzy. Each came from his own personal choice. Each had a need, a problem, a care and worry. When they gathered all in one place, Jesus had all their sorrows lumped together. No wonder He felt pity.

Application

Gather up all your cares. Reflect on all your anxieties. When they come to you one by one, you don't realize how burdened you are. As you put them together, you can see why you are weighed down and why you need Jesus.

139

"Dismiss the crowds so that they may go to the villages and buy some food for themselves." (V-15)

Thought

This solution has human dimensions. It is the prudent, sure, thought out way to handle the problem. That is never enough. Jesus asks the Apostles to believe. God always wants to provide. When the goal is difficult or impossible, He asks a special faith.

Application

After you have done everything possible, place each situation in God's hands. Otherwise, anxiety takes over and you are paralyzed. As you believe, God's power c can enter. He can bless your works and your life's toil. Works, great and small, demand that you trust God's power.

"There is no need for them to disperse." (V-16)

Thought

People quit too soon. Works are begun with enthusiasm. The goal seems so near. Then the person sees the road is longer than expected. The bodily and emotional forces are drained. The goal fades. The temptation to quit grows. At this moment, faith in Jesus is needed.

Application

Don't spend your life building unfinished houses in which no one can live. Bring your tasks to a completion. To do this you have to believe, especially when unforeseen problems arise. At these moments, stop and call upon Jesus. He will tell you not to disperse what you have gathered.

"I am sure of this much; that He who has begun the good work in you will carry it through to completion, right up to the day of Christ Jesus." (Phil:1-6)

"Bring them here." (V-18)

Thought

Jesus wants everything in His hands. Already the Father has given Him all. His hands do whatever is needed - healing, multiplying, even raising from the dead. His crucified hands are now glorified, manifesting the Resurrection power of His wounds.

Application

How do you put everything in Jesus' hands? Just mentally take your cares, anxieties, hopes and dreams and give them to Jesus. Be careful not to take them back! Then, Jesus will show you what to do. He will tell you whose help to seek or how to handle the difficulty.

All those present ate their fill. (V-20)

Thought

Jesus takes care of everyone. He excludes no one from the banquet. All can eat.

The world keeps it's privileges for the few. In the world there are "haves" and "have nots." In the Kingdom, all are "haves" to the fullest.

Application

Don't think the Kingdom isn't for you. Jesus feeds everyone. The Father has abundantly provided. Don't say you are unworthy, or not as good as others. Approach Jesus' table and ask for His food.

CHAPTER 43
A NIGHT ON THE LAKE (14:22-36)

Jesus insisted that his disciples get into the boat and precede him to the other side. (V-22)

Thought

People always think of a gentle Jesus. However, Jesus was never gentle about the Father's will. Jesus knew the disciples were supposed to get into the boat. A powerful manifestation was imminent.

God's powerful works are preceded by people knowing His will. His works go undone, because too many don't know God's will. People don't even think it is important to know His will.

Application

Do you seek God's will? Do you know God's will for you? You, like everyone in God's world, are called. God's call is no hidden mystery. God freely and openly reveals to you. You have to search and want to know.

He went up on the mountain by himself to pray. (V-23)

Thought

The mountain, being that part of earth closest to the heavens, is a natural symbol of prayer. Climbing the mountain shows the person's desire to speak with God. The mountain symbol represents the minutes given to rising above the tasks and cares, freeing the mind for God. So few know God's will because they don't climb the mountain of prayer everyday.

Application

Do you go up that mountain, by yourself, everyday? Do you find just a few minutes to stop and think of

142

God? You can do it anywhere. Walking along, sitting in a chair, or riding a bus. This book is meant to help you get used to daily, spiritual mountain climbing.

At about three in the morning, he came walking toward them on the lake. (V-25)

Thought

Jesus shows up in the strangest places! The apostles thought He was on the mountain. Instead He comes to them. Why this strange manifestation, walking on the water at 3:00 A.M.? Maybe to console those who still find themselves awake at 3:00 A.M.? Probably to console everyone being tossed about by life's waves. In the strangest places, at the least probable time, just when people are despairing, Jesus comes.

Application

You associate Jesus with Church and an ordered life, not with 3:00 A.M. visits. Jesus comes to you in the very disordered moments of life. When you don't want anything to do with the gospels; when you've seemingly broken all the rules; when you are empty and lonely, Jesus comes.

"Get hold of yourselves! It is I. Do not be afraid." (V-27)

Thought

Jesus comes in disordered moments, when everything is coming apart. In this verse, Jesus makes three claims: "By my power, this disordered life will be turned around." "I didn't send an angel, I came myself." "You are used to living in fear, but that fear is over." How can He make those claims in such moments of personal disarray? Because the Father has given Him all power and authority.

143

Application

You need to hear all three parts. Do you want to give up your disordered life style? Do you believe Jesus comes to you? Finally, can you let go of your fears, and accept Jesus' power over you?

"Come!" he said. So Peter got out of the boat and began to walk on the water. (V-29)

Thought

Jesus speaks one word, "Come." He completely changed a fearful man into someone ready to undertake an incredible challenge. The change was instant. Peter listened to no sermons! Attended no weekend retreat! He heard one word from Jesus.

Application

You, too, can be freed instantaneously. Whether it is a small problem that's been there for years, or an insurmountable difficulty, it doesn't matter. One word from Jesus is enough. Continue to believe. You will experience the moment when Jesus says, "Come."

"How little faith you have!" (V-31)

Thought

Some people are able to believe in a crisis but can't walk in faith. They can't take the daily steps. Possibly they have experienced the faith moment of "being born again." But that moment passes and they don't live on in that new life.

Application

Have you experienced a faith moment? Were you faithful to that experience? Did you keep your eyes on Jesus? Does the power of Jesus remain with you?

Those who were in the boat showed him reverence. (V-33)

Thought

They hadn't wandered out, or faltered, or been picked up again like Peter. They were still eyewitnesses to Jesus' power. He never invited all to come out on the waters. He provided their faith experience by letting them sit in the boat.

Application

You don't have to do extraordinary deeds to receive faith. You just have to be obedient to God's will. You have to get into the boat that Jesus wants you in. Once in, just sit there. The rest is God's job.

CHAPTER 44
TOTAL HONESTY (15:1-20)

"Why do you for your part act contrary to the commandment of God for the sake of your tradition." (V-3)

Thought

Even the official translation puts tradition in quotation marks, pointing out that the word is used by Jesus with tongue in check. The tradition is obviously wrong, and should be clearly seen as contrary to God's law. What does it take to show these people their mistakes? They cling to false ideas that support their own tendencies.

Application

Do you cling, also, to thoughts, prejudices, ambitions and desires that are against God's commandments? Will you let go? Will you allow God's word to have control? You can't cling to your own "traditions" and at the same time, possess Jesus.

145

"This means that for the sake of your tradition you have nullified God's word." (V-6)

Thought

What an accusation - that they have nullified God's word. Nullify means nothing is left. *What once was* now has no power. Imagine nullifying God's word. Where does a person go after that? Nothing is left. God's word, meant to bring to salvation, no longer has power.

Application

How do you see God's word? As an intruder into your life? How do you feel about God's word? Better off without it? Or, do you want God's word? Do you seek and welcome it? According to Paul, the gospel "is the power of God, leading everyone who believes in it to salvation..." (Rom 1:16). How you internally approach that word is your salvation or condemnation.

"This people pays me lip service but their heart is far from me." (V-7)

Thought

A person should be one. The mind, heart, and body should all be going in the same direction. That's called "truth" and simplicity. Here we have duality. The body's members go in different directions. The tongue so easily says "Yes, Lord" but the heart has its own agenda.

Application

Do not let your tongue lie to you. You can speak fine words about your love for God, and then mistakenly believe that your own words are true. Rather, speak few words. In the quiet you can examine where your heart really is.

"It is not what goes into a man's mouth that makes him impure; it is what comes out of his mouth." (V-11)

Thought

Food seems so real. Words so unimportant. Yet Jesus sees differently. The God relationship has little to do with food and much to do with the words.

Application

How many words will you speak? All kinds will come from your mouth. Words of gossip; of revealing faults; of untruths; of ambition and greed; of getting your own way; and expressing your own opinion. You should change all that. Begin first with your heart.

"Every planting not put down by my heavenly Father will be uprooted." (V-13)

Thought

This planting is God's word within. People scandalized by this word have no accepting hearts for the seed. They block the word, screening out it's power, and refusing to let the message change their lives. Like rain upon cement, the water can't sink in.

Application

What inner attitudes do you bring to Jesus' message? Jesus constantly asks that question. What goes on in your heart? What thoughts, feelings and attitudes do you bring? So much depends on that.

"If one blind man leads another, both will end in a pit." (V-14)

Thought

If both the teacher and the student don't know where they are going, what good is that school? Better for it to be closed down! Every religious teacher shouldn't be followed. Some lead people to confusion and destruction where the fruit or the seed is destroyed.

Application
You have the Church. You have those trained and accepted for ministry. You have books, acclaimed for centuries as safe guides to religious questions. You have sound, spiritual traditions. No need to end up in a religious pit.

"...what comes out of the mouth originates in the mind?" (V-18)

Thought
Jesus keeps getting inside. So many would stop short, content with external practices, totally unmindful of the world within. Jesus preceded the dynamic psychologists by centuries. He always preached the importance of the hidden thoughts and covered-over ambitions.

Application
In coming to know Jesus, you will also see yourself. You will see the good and the bad. Both are there. The Spirit fosters the good, and reduces the evil tendencies within. You have to be honest about both to accept the Spirit's full power.

CHAPTER 45
THE ONE AND THE MANY (15:21-31)

"Lord, Son of David, have pity on me!" (V-22)

Thought

She probably felt that using the title would help. She would use anything that would release His powers. So, she gave Him a great title and lowered herself to seek His gifts. Her goal was clear - that Jesus could recognize her and change her condition.

Application

Keep your goal clear to have God's help in your life. His power can change anything, so bring your problems to Him. Don't turn away. Don't grow discouraged. Don't say that He doesn't hear. At the right moment in the right way, His power will come to you.

He gave her no word of response. (V-23)

Thought

That seems the same result as our own prayers. So many words go up to heaven, but so few words seemingly come down. Yet every word is heard. Every plea is counted. There must be something we don't understand yet. It will be revealed as we keep pleading.

Application

Never stop asking and pleading, even if there seems "no word of response." The very pleading makes you holy and keeps your eyes on God. If you received your gift too quickly, you would wander off, completely forgetting what was given and Who bestowed it.

"My mission is only to the lost sheep of the house of Israel." (V-24)

Thought

This statement highlights the contradiction. Jesus reserves Himself for the Jews, but the Jews don't want Him. Later Jesus will give Himself totally for His people and send the apostles first to them. Their rejection is clear, because their opportunities are total.

Application

Possibly from earliest years you have learned of Jesus. Over and again the chances to know Him have been present. Jesus lives entirely for you. He gave you the Church, the Eucharist, and these Scriptures. All around you are His saving helps. He needs you to accept His gifts.

"It is not right to take the food of sons and daughters and throw it to the dogs." (V-26)

Thought

Jesus speaks as if His healing powers were limited. Whatever time He gave to the woman would be stolen from the Jews! No one can say He wasn't loyal to His people. Yet He expected loyalty in return.

Application

How loyal Jesus has been to you! Even when you strayed, He went after you. When you got involved with other pursuits He patiently waited.

Delay no longer. His full giving demands your full surrender. He rightly expects your complete loyalty.

"Woman, you have great faith!" (V-28)

Thought

Finally Jesus breaks down His defense. He allows the woman's personal faith to overcome His ideas of His mission to the Jews. What she wasn't by nature (a child of the promise), she became by faith. This little scene foretold the vast opening to the Gentile world where faith admitted millions to Jesus, even though nature made them only Gentiles.

Application

Your faith roots you in the Davidic line, even though you are Gentile. A great mystery here! Jesus the Nazarene, is for everyone. Call upon His name, His power is yours. This poor woman broke through. You can follow her. Jesus is for everyone, Jew or Greek, salve or free, male or female.

The result was great astonishment in the crowds. (V-31)

Thought

The gospel crowds have simplicity. They don't stop to think, or to question. They quickly move into faith. Jesus, in turn, loved them. When the Pharisees or Scribes raised questions, He would make His teaching to the whole crowd, knowing He would get a fair hearing.

Application

Imitate the good qualities here. Move quickly into faith. Give Jesus' words a fair hearing. Don't be questioning or captious. The Kingdom is at hand. To delay can mean to lose out.

They glorified the God of Israel. (V-31)

Thought

The crowds did not hold back the praise or the "Hosannas." Later, they would enthusiastically lay

151

palms and welcome Jesus to Jerusalem. The crowds didn't keep things to themselves. They let Jesus know their feelings.

Application
How did you glorify God this day? What words came to your lips? Blessings or curses? God's name in praise or in vain? The heart changes the speech, but speech confirms and strengthens what is happening inside. You can't live spiritually within and refuse to glorify God externally.

CHAPTER 46
THE BEGINNING ATTITUDE
(15:32-36; 16:1-12)

"How could we ever get enough bread in this deserted spot to satisfy such a crowd?" (V-33)

Thought
Certain people measure their human talents and calculate what they can do for God. That's not the way at all. Others, with few human talents, look only at Jesus - at His power and His love for the people. They do wonderful works, far beyond what anyone could expect.

Application
First, let Jesus stir up your desires to do good. Then be still, keeping our eye on Him. Events will occur. Hopes and dreams will begin within you. Then, you will find yourself doing a great work in Jesus' power.

After giving thanks he broke them and gave them to the disciples. (V-36)

Thought

Jesus never wanted to be the star. He gladly shared the work and spotlight with the disciples. This miracle literally took place in the disciples' hands and Jesus rejoiced to share His powers.

Application

By your Baptism you share all of Jesus' powers. No longer limited to the one place or even to a mortal body. His body is now mystical. The Kingdom has come. Let Jesus use your human nature to do all the works He used to do through His physical body.

The Pharisees and Sadducees came along, and as a test asked him to show them some sign in the sky. (V-1)

Thought

The sky seems untouchable to human power. So they sought an ultimate sign, something definitely from God. What would they do if they received it? Why didn't the already present signs suffice? Who were they to call the shots and determine the rules?

Application

You have to begin correctly. You are not in charge. You don't call the shots. You don't say how events should go.

Instead, you rejoice to be in the Kingdom. You praise God and seek His will. You don't claim to know everything. You do realize that God's mysteries are beyond you, especially His love for you.

"An evil, faithless age is eager for a sign." (V-4)

Thought

Can the blind see a beautiful painting, or the deaf hear a symphony? Unfortunately, they don't have capable

153

eyes or ears. So, there must be something in our hearts *before* we can hear God's message.

Application
Rather than let yourself seek signs, believe and wait and seek.

Seeking signs begets impatience, criticism, cynicism, and a readiness to give up easily. No one can grasp the Kingdom with those dispositions.

"Be on the lookout against the yeast of the Pharisees and Sadducees." (V-6)

Thought
Jesus doesn't want these wrong attitudes spreading to the disciples. If so, the Kingdom would never take root.

They could be easily fooled, trading in their simple faith for religious sophistication. In that trade they would lose the Kingdom's power.

Application
Don't let yourself be fooled. In the religious world, many people use many words, but they cannot produce faith. Others with just a few words, touch hearts and bring all close to God. Seek the simple faith and avoid religious quarrels.

"Do you not remember the five loaves among five thousand and how many baskets-full you picked up? (V-9)

Thought
God's works shouldn't be quickly relegated to the forgotten past. Recalling them brings power. Human friendships are built on memories. True friends always remember.

154

Here, Jesus stokes the embers of memory to rekindle the faith of that moment. These words stir up for the disciples the same feelings they had when they gathered up the fragments.

Application
Take a moment to recall what God has done for you. Begin with your earliest years. As you go over the memories, you will see God's hand even more clearly than you did at the time.

He was always there - in your decisions, in your opportunities, in preventing you from foolish actions, and in giving you wisdom.

"...I was not speaking about bread at all but warning you against the yeast of the Pharisees?" (V-11)

Thought
The small yeast affects everything. In this case, the yeast spoils God's work, not allowing the Pharisees to hear the message.

The crowds, with no religious training caught the message clearly, but this yeast was hindering the Pharisees.

Application
Do you have any block to Jesus? Does anything spoil His work, or always gets in the way?

It's important that you understand your own "yeast" and not allow its power to ruin the Kingdom within you

CHAPTER 47
THE BASIC QUESTION (16:13-20)

"Who do people say that the Son of Man is?" (V-13)

Thought

The most important question in the world's history. A question for everyone born into this world.

The question was spoken softly, without much drama. The words themselves needed no dramatic buildup. They are a door, about to be opened for the first time.

Application

Whom do you say Jesus is? Have you even asked that question? Do you see its importance? Or to you is this just one of the many questions in life?

"Some say John the Baptizer, others Elijah, still others Jeremiah or one of the prophets." (V-14)

Thought

These answers represent the world's wisdom. They are wrong. This is typical because the world has answers to everything. Ask the world "What is important?" or "What comes first?" And answers will be quickly given, all of them wrong.

Application

Before knowing it, you are swept up in the world. The TV soap operas, the mass media, the latest fashion, the newest star. All is whirlwind, not giving you time even to ask the important question. So be still. Turn off the television and let the Kingdom come to you. Ask the important question.

"And you," he said to them, "who do you say that I am?" (V-15)

Thought

Jesus reminded them of the original question, which they tried to escape by quoting others. He won't let them sidestep this question. He wants them to search their own hearts; reflect on their own experiences; and face their own responsibility for this question.

Application

You have to answer this for yourself. You can't say "Well, so and so thinks this." You have a responsibility to answer, "Who is Jesus Christ?"

Don't run away. Don't think you can put the question off until tomorrow. Answer the question now and being a new life.

"You are the Messiah," Simon Peter answered, "The Son of the living God." (V-18)

Thought

For thousands of years, Jewish people looked for the Messiah. Now, near Caesarea Philippi, Peter was saying this man was He.

Application

Jesus comes to you at a definite place, time and circumstance. Yours is not the same as Peter's. However, the gift is the same when the answer comes forth. The Father will reveal to you who Jesus is.

"No mere man has revealed this to you, but my heavenly Father." (V-18)

Thought

The Father delights in revealing His Son. In our hearts, He opens to us the mystery. "This is My Son," He says.

157

Every day, in many hearts, people experience the gift of knowing who Jesus is.

Application
You don't have to go to Caesarea Philippi. The gospel message has come to you. Just read the pages. Take in the mystery. Ask the Father to enlighten you. This gift is everywhere for everyone - to come to know God's Son.

"...you are 'Rock', and on this rock I will build my church..." (V-18)

Thought
Two thousand years ago, these men stood with Jesus. The promise has been kept. The Church continues. The Rock survives, imbedded in the mystery of Jesus.

Application
You will survive in one place - rooted in the Church that is founded upon rock. You need a visible Church. You can't find Jesus only in your Bible. You need a living tradition and a community of believers.

"...the jaws of death shall not prevail against it." (V-18)

Thought
It's no fun to be caught in the jaws of death. Yet death surrounds life. Powerful forces are everywhere. Daily realities. Ask anyone who has experienced them. Against all of this, the rock prevails.

Application
Each day you face the "jaws of death" - the perils all around. If you escape today, who will guarantee your escape tomorrow? The promise is made to the Church. So stay within the Church and experience its protection.

From then on Jesus (the Messiah) started to indicate to his disciples that he must go to Jerusalem and suffer. (V-21)

Thought

"Started to indicate" means two things. First, Jesus understood that He couldn't reveal this all at once. Secondly, the disciples couldn't yet accept the cross.

Since everything was going so well, why did Jesus introduce these thoughts now? They seemed so out of tune. Yet the words had to be said.

Application

At certain times, you don't want to hear, you don't even want to face the truth. Yet, you have to listen.

You aren't free to do everything you want. You can't have a family and act like a "single." You have certain burdens to carry, and responsibilities to face. Jesus has some words for you, so listen.

...and raised up on the third day. (V-21)

Thought

Jesus says this as calmly as the rest of the sentence. As surely as He knew His death, He also knew His resurrection. Many great people foresaw their death. They could see the enemies plotting and the inevitable moment coming closer. Jesus went much further. He knew that the Father would intervene. Accepting death takes great faith, but believing in God's power three days later, goes beyond human faith.

Application
You are invited into Jesus' faith. You should believe that you will rise in glory with Jesus. He went first so you can follow, knowing that He awaits you.

At this, Peter took him aside and began to remonstrate with him. (V-22)

Thought
Peter must have only heard the first part of the sentence. He never bothered to ask what "being raised up on the third day" meant. Instead he was concerned about the suffering.

Application
Don't be discouraged by the gospel teaching about the cross. Suffering can discourage you and make you forget that the Father will raise you up.

No one can endure life's sufferings without God's help. So think more about the helping Father than about the problem of suffering.

"God forbid that any such thing ever happen to you!" (V-22)

Thought
Peter must have thought that Jesus was just going to glide right through life, as if His glory was going to come cheaply. Where would that leave all of His followers who would have to shed their blood?

Jesus suffered to help us with our suffering. He accepted the suffering moments because they are part of everyone's life.

Application

Jesus is near to you. Your suffering moments are difficult - the broken heart, the ruined hopes, even the broken and sickly body. Jesus had moments of all those. He is with you in your suffering moments. That's the Jesus mystery.

"Get out of my sight, you satan!" (V-23)

Thought

Strong words, but the temptation to run away from suffering is also strong. People isolate themselves, putting up defenses to avoid suffering.

It happens every day. People avoid certain people. Refuse to face some issues. Cut corners on responsibility. Let fears dominate them - all to avoid suffering at any cost.

Application

Face the flight from suffering within you. It's a powerful temptation, leading to lies, dishonesty and selfishness. Accept today's little suffering. It won't ruin you. At the end of the day, you will have faced the troubles honestly.

"Whoever would save his life will lose it, but whoever loses his life for my sake will find it." (V-25)

Thought

No one "has" their own life. Life is handed to us moment by moment. We have no choice except to give it away. Who can stop time? Who has total control over the body's aging process? Who is immune from death?

The wise person sees that life passes, whether he chooses or not, so he gives his life away for Jesus' sake.

161

Application
*Don't grasp. Don't hold on. Don't deceive yourself
that you have your whole life ahead. You have only
this moment and it quickly passes away for the next
moment.*

*Give your life away to Jesus. He created time! Only
He can gather up your moments and keep them for the
Kingdom.*

> ### "What profit would a man show if he were
> ### to gain the whole world
> ### and destroy himself in the process?" (V-26)

Thought
Compare one rational human person to all the rest of
material creation. The one person is greater. There are
more worlds in his thought that in all the stars and
planets. And they, too, will pass away!

So every person should choose the life placed within by
the Father over any part of creation, even the whole
world.

Application
*Learn what is important! Not material things or
worldly fame or power or anything else the world can
give.*

*What the Father has placed within you is important.
The Kingdom of God is there. Don't gamble your
inner, lasting gift for anything in the world.*

CHAPTER 49
ON THE MOUNTAIN (17:1-13)

...Jesus took Peter, James and his brother John... (V-1)

Thought

It is a joy just to be with Jesus. To be singled for apostleship is unique. To be among the closest of apostles, the greatest privilege. These three realized the special gift even before this mountain trip. After they came down, no words could explain the gift of being with Him.

Application

You, called into the kingdom, enjoy the same gift. You can't understand or comprehend the privilege. No one does or can. However, you can grow in that understanding. You should grow. You are called to grasp the mystery.

He was transfigured before their eyes... (V-2)

Thought

Jesus is the Kingdom. As far as possible, the Kingdom is now revealed. The gospel says "before their eyes," but the gift touched every faculty, - mind, emotions, will and imagination. They had a searing religious experience, hidden to the outside world by silence but never forgotten within.

Application

This gift is your prayer model. In prayer, Jesus calls you to the mountain. By setting aside your daily routine, you accept that call. Within your heart's stillness, Jesus is revealed in a quiet, momentary religious experience. Listen to that call often today.

...Lord, how good that we are here! (V-4)

Thought

Peter often made dumb responses, but these words were perfect. He grasped quickly that God's power was all around him. The next verses show that he spoke too quickly, because the Father was about to speak.

Application

Be still in prayer. Wait until the gift is complete. Don't rush, don't think the beginning experience is everything. God wants to reveal Himself to you. That takes time. His action is limited by our hurrying. Your prayers should be more than a few hurried thoughts. Otherwise your relationship to God is superficial.

...the disciples fell forward on the ground overcome with fear. (V-6)

Thought

The experience proves too strong, too overwhelming. The veil is drawn back. For a moment they see clearly. They see Jesus and the Kingdom. It is too much for them. They will never be the same again. They can never forget. They have seen what prophets and kings never saw. Religious experiences always leave their mark.

Application

You are called to the same prayer. The gift is for everyone now. You are called to the mountain, to see Jesus and to experience the Kingdom. Open yourself to the gift. Let the Spirit come. You won't be the same. The experience will change you.

...Do not tell anyone of the vision until the Son of Man rises from the dead. (V-9)

Thought

The event wasn't to be tomorrow's headlines. Jesus is not passing news, but the permanent good news. This experience is for all the world. Everyone will be invited to the mountain when the Spirit Comes. Only after the Resurrection, will that invitation go forth.

Application

Now is the time. The gospel story is your invitation. Jesus is God's Son. He knows the Father and will gladly reveal the Father to you. You need only the Spirit to help you. He knows the way up the mountain. When he takes you there, you will see Jesus.

...Why do the scribes claim that "Elijah" must come first? (V-10)

Thought

Some people always complicate prayer. They tell others not to expect much at a beginner's stage. They say that certain conditions have to be fulfilled before God bestows the mountain-top experience. They are always wrong, sending people away discouraged.

Application

Don't limit Jesus. Don't think you can't pray until you fast or become holy. You must start with Jesus. You must begin on the mountain-top. Don't complicate your prayer. Don't try to fulfill conditions. Begin. Seek Jesus. Expect the prayer gift.

...that Elijah has already come, but they did not recognize him. (V-12)

Thought

The Jews always believed that Elijah had to return before the Messiah would come. With one sentence, the disciples realized now that He was already in their midst.

165

Application
Let the scales fall from your eyes. Jesus is already in your midst. He doesn't wait until you are holy or sinless or perfect or even going in the right direction. You don't have to get into a church building or even get your life in order. He comes now! Nothing stands in His way.

CHAPTER 50
MOUNTAIN MOVING FAITH (17:14-27)

"Lord," he said, "take pity on my son, who is demented and in a serious condition." (V-15)

Thought
Some people claim that Jesus' power in all these stories was just "persuasion healing" of illnesses that would be diagnosed today by modern medicine. It's true that the gospel writers weren't trained psychiatrists. They looked at the problems in a common sense way. However, the problems seemed real (whatever their source). The son is in *serious condition*. Jesus Himself never diagnosed. He just healed.

Application
Jesus' power is real. No matter what your problems are, even if you see yourself in serious condition, His power is for you. Jesus doesn't just heal your little problems. He touches every problem.

"I have brought him to our disciples but they could not cure him." (V-16)

Thought
The man had stopped short of Jesus. He had gone only as far as the disciples. He was just now approaching

the only Healer. The power of God was released when he came to Jesus.

Application
Don't come up short. Don't just read about healings. Don't think they are associated with certain places. Don't believe that healings just come through certain people. So cry out! Don't stop short - Go to Jesus!

Then Jesus reprimanded him, and the demon came out of him. (V-18)

Thought
There are two *"hims"* in that verse, but they refer to different beings. The first *him* means satan. The second *him* means the child. Within everyone is a similar confusion. Many times people feel they are not really "themselves." They can't get rid of fear, anxiety, compulsive behavior, worry, etc.

Application
Those feelings are not the real you, so don't accept them. Seek to be freed from them. Let Jesus reprimand them. Jesus wants to cleanse you and then clothe you. Certain feelings have to "come out" of you. You should be released from them by Jesus.

"Why could we not expel it?" (V-19)

Thought
That's a question every healer and exorcist has asked. Jesus' gift was always effective. Whenever he asked or commanded, changes came. No one else ever had these gifts to that degree.

Application
Don't be discouraged by your imperfect religious gifts. Be instead a little child, knowing that your gifts will be

stronger and greater tomorrow. What power you have isn't important. What power Jesus gives you is very important.

"Because you have so little trust." (V-20)

Thought

Jesus unveils the secret of His power. The answer is simple, but people still don't understand. They want to know just how He does it. Instead He says "you have so little trust." If people took those words, and listened to them in their hearts, then they wouldn't fail.

Application

When you accept the truth, that trusting God is vital, you will be walking the right path. Trust isn't one of many virtues. Trust is all the virtues wrapped together. Trust isn't one road to God. It's the only road. So start trusting God with all your heart.

"...if you had faith the size of a mustard seed, nothing would be impossible for you." (V-20)

Thought

If some fanatic said those words, then people would easily write them off. But Jesus said them. Two words are important - "nothing" and "impossible." They don't allow an escape or an exception.

Application

Everywhere, you see problems - to your health, your family, your economic position, your purpose in life, to everything. Here Jesus says "nothing is impossible." Then, take your problems to Him. You're sure His first words will be "that is not impossible..." Let Jesus show you how He will do the impossible.

168

At these words they were overwhelmed with grief. (V-23)

Thought

Jesus just finished telling them that nothing was impossible and already grief overwhelms them. They couldn't shake the feelings. They seemed powerless in it's grasp. This beautiful story will end in tragedy. It's all over. The Son of Man is going to be delivered.

Application

You know this problem is real. This is not a movie. It's real life, "Putting Him to death" will be real. But does another reality exist? An untouchable reality called eternal life? Every suffering and destruction is real. But for those who love God, death is not the final reality. Grief can't totally claim anyone who believes in the Kingdom.

CHAPTER 51
THE LITTLE CHILD (18:1-14)

"Who is of greatest importance in the kingdom of God?" (V-1)

Thought

The question is excellent, but the disciples didn't understand what to seek. To them, the Kingdom of God was an earthly reality, with all the trappings of power and fame. They weren't ready yet for the full revelation of the Kingdom.

Application

You know that His Kingdom is unseen, and that you will experience it fully after death. Yet, much of the disciples' foolishness clings to you. You still chase after power, fortune, fame, a good name - all the seen and visible goals. Seek, instead, the true Kingdom, perceived by faith.

"I assure you, unless you change and become like little children, you will not enter the kingdom of God." (V-3)

Thought
This shatters everything. Earthly kingdoms are seized by the mature and powerful. What can a little child possess? What kind of Kingdom is this? The disciples have a hard time even understanding this teaching.

Application
You still have much to learn about the Kingdom. You have to cast aside worldly learning. You grew up in the world. You think and feel like the world. You have to think differently to grasp the Kingdom.

"Whoever makes himself lowly, becoming like this child, is of greatest importance in that heavenly reign." (V-4)

Thought
A child had no rights. He was the property of parents. A child, then, meant a complete giving up of worldly rights and protection, knowing that the heavenly Father provides everything. As the disciples became empty of earthly rights and privileges, their share in the Kingdom increased.

Application
Where do you want to be important? In the Kingdom or on earth? You can't have both. You can't cling to worldly honors; you can't seek man's esteem and still be of importance in the Kingdom.

"Whoever welcomes one such child for my sake welcomes me." (V-5)

Thought

When a person gives up earthly privileges, the Father provides - often through others who themselves are rewarded. The Kingdom, then, is a system just like the world, but with many differences. All are cared for and none are discarded. People seek to help others, not to be served.

Application

You cannot be a Christian by yourself. You need others and they need you. You cannot overcome the world's system without the Kingdom's system of relationships according to the gospel. Let the Kingdom begin within you and start looking for others who also treasure that Kingdom.

"What terrible things will come on the world through scandal!" (V-7)

Thought

"Scandal" is always happening through people who have only worldly standards. They do everything the "world's way." This then becomes the behavioral norm. This "scandal" is only broken by the Kingdom's power entering and showing a better way.

Application

If your behavior is untouched by the gospel, then you too are a scandal. You act, think, feel and live like the world. You learn behavior and pass on behavior that doesn't reflect the Kingdom. Let the Kingdom come into your life, so you stop being a scandal to the little ones.

"If your hand or foot is your undoing, cut it off and throw it from you. Better to enter life maimed or crippled than be thrown with two hands or two feet into endless fire." (V-8)

Thought
Seemingly an extreme statement! But what price can be put on eternal life? What compares to being God's child and the Kingdom's member? Giving up life is not too high a price.

Application
Set your values right. Nothing should come before the Kingdom. Nothing should keep you out of the Kingdom. If anything stands between you and the Kingdom, let go. Give it up. Throw it overboard.

"I assure you, their angels in heaven constantly behold my heavenly Father's face." (V-10)

Thought
What's it like to behold the Father's face? Jesus knew what it was like. All the saints and angels also know. Seeing that face, they are always helping us, to whom that vision is still veiled. One day, the vision will be ours, also.

Application
Do you ever dream of yourself "seeing God" or actually being in heaven? It seems so far away. Yet think of all your loved ones who have gone before you. You know they are there, for they persevered in faith. You will be with them some day.

CHAPTER 52

THE CHRISTIAN GATHERING
(18:15-20)

"If your brother should commit some wrong against you, go and point out his fault, but keep it between the two of you." (V-15)

Thought

People usually do just the opposite. They don't point out the fault but tell everyone except the person. Jesus asks for a complete reversal. He wants honesty and then silence. Honesty with the brother so the sin can be corrected. Silence to protect his good name. Otherwise the person continues in his fault and the evil is multiplied by the tongue.

Application

Be honest in your speech. Say words that will help, guide and correct. Everyone depends on those words. Then be silent, not sharing the fault with everyone. If you speak you just tickle people's ears and hurt even your listeners.

"If he does not listen, summon another..." (V-16)

Thought

"Summoning another" shows that the Early Church took *fault correcting* as important. All knew the perfection they were called to, and the need for fraternal correction. Today, little true correction goes on. People allow others to go downhill without a word. Some slip into serious abuses and not a word is said. All are afraid to "hurt their feelings." Instead, they let them risk losing the Kingdom.

Application

Fulfilling this command of Jesus, won't win you popularity contests. Many aren't ready to accept

fraternal correction. Yet, the words have to be said.
Correcting words give the person a chance to change.
If the case is serious, then two should approach the
person.

"If he ignores them, refer it to the church." (V-17)

Thought

People are not saved once and for all. God's saving act
puts people on salvation's road. They must choose to
continue. Here, the Church as the ultimate criterion,
comes on the scene. The whole local assembly faces
the question. If they are not listened to, then the person
must leave the community.

Application

Begin, as the text says, with individual honesty,
including others who might be some help. Finally
appeal to the parish, if need be. Seek out the priest
and, if necessary, let him judge. After that, you have
done everything possible.

"...whatever you declare bound on earth shall be held bound in heaven..." (V-18)

Thought

We tend to see *bound* as negative, referring this part to
unforgiven sins. But certain things should be "bound."
It's good to be bound to agreements to our word and
promises. It's good to be bound with others in Christian
community. These bonds of agreements, promises and
relationships are blessed by God.

Application

Christ sets you free but He doesn't set you loose, able to
wander as you please. If you are never "bound" you
can't be part of His building or His body. So ask where
God calls you to be "bound." What commitment should
you make? That's your calling, your vocation.

174

"...whatever you declare loosed on earth shall be held loosed in heaven." (V-18)

Thought

Individually, a person declares others loosed when he forgives. By forgiving, the person surrenders his right to reparation, thus loosing the other. The Church does the same, especially in the Sacrament of Reconciliation. On earth, individuals or organizations are always doing this. Prison boards grant paroles. Governments reduce back taxes.

By faith, a person believes that the Father forgives in heaven. With Jesus' promise, we know what goes on in the Father's mind.

Application

Forgive all who have hurt you. Hold no grudges. Hold nothing against anyone. When you do this, you will find new freedom. For the Father forgives you also.

"...if two of you join your voices on earth to pray for anything whatever, it shall be granted you by my Father in heaven." (V-19)

Thought

In this text the Church isn't solving disputes but seeking gifts. Jesus promises even the smallest Christian community (two of you) unlimited intercessory powers. Unfortunately, people often join together only in a crisis. Or worse, many try to find God's gifts by themselves.

Application

With whom do you pray? With whom do you join "your voice on earth?" If no one, then something is missing. You will be a full Christian only in community, even if this community is only yourself and another. Go and

175

seek a Christian prayer partner, someone with a heart similar to yours. Then, join your voices.

"Where two or three are gathered in my name, there am I in their midst." (V-20)

Thought
Man is a social animal, naturally gathering into groups. The world gathers people into companies, schools, institutions. People gather together for entertainment, profit or common goals. The Christian gathering is different. People gather in Jesus' name. When they gather the Kingdom is present and God acts.

Application
Don't miss opportunities to gather in His name - at the parish liturgy, in family prayer, or even with just one other person. Whenever you gather, Jesus comes. The world gathers for is goals. You must gather so God can do His work in you.

CHAPTER 53
FORGIVEN BUT UNFORGIVING
(18:21-35)

"...not seven times: I say, seventy times seven times." (V-22)

Thought
How can Jesus expect such unlimited forgiveness? Isn't there a time to strike back? To stop the forgiveness and tell the person that this is the last time? Human nature doesn't understand. The Father takes care of His little ones; protects those who forgive; and forgives whoever pardons.

Application

You won't learn forgiveness lessons from the world. Forgiving comes only from believing in the Father whom Jesus preached. Only the Kingdom has power to remove anger and to heal hostility. Let that power come to you right now. Right now in your hearts forgive whoever has wronged you.

"...like a king who decided to settle accounts with his officials." (V-23)

Thought

The day of "settling accounts" always comes. The accounts are added. The book is closed and the total given to Jesus.

Application

These simple truths touch deep beliefs. Are you caught up in this world? Do you see rank, fame and prestige as vital? What do you value, - worldly gain or the Father's love? Into which account do you store your treasure?

When he began his auditing, one was brought in who owed him a huge amount. (V-24)

Thought

We are that person. We all owe God a huge amount. We were purchased at a great price, and are totally unable to repay. We owe Jesus everything. We owe the Father because He sent Jesus. We owe the Spirit who is given abundantly and freely. We are all the world's greatest debtors.

Application

Don't look at your good deeds and feel that you don't owe God that much. Look at the treasures that He gave you which you could never purchase. These gifts are the one necessary treasure - eternal life.

"My lord, be patient with me, and I will pay you back in full." (V-26)

Thought

When would he ever be able to "pay back in full?" He probably couldn't even keep up the interest payments. He was going to lose everything and be cast into jail. Yet the Lord accepts his plea at face value, not even asking any details. The supposed change of heart suffices.

Application

You feel your prayers are said with little faith. Yet even these prayers are not lost. The Father searches for any excuse to respond. Even at the prayers' beginning the gifts are made ready. You can never "pay back in full," so seek God's mercy.

...let the official go and wrote off the debt. (V-27)

Thought

To postpone or even to diminish the debt would be merciful. To write off the debt is extravagance. Total mercy, that is the Father. People can't grasp that. They think He haggles and barters and measures. Really, He just forgives. Scandalous! Too easy! Too good to be true! But the gospel says He "wrote off the debt."

Application

He will write off your debt. So, gather up all your debts (like someone going to a loan company), all the failures, all your sins, the serious ones and the slight ones. The Father wants to write them all off. Right now! Don't even say you will "pay Him back in full." You can't. God wants to pour out His mercy. He only wants you to know that you have debts.

Instead he had him put in jail until he paid back what he owed. (V-30)

Thought

The man forgot. He was forgiven everything and he quickly forgot. He acted as if he had paid back; as if no one had even canceled his debt. He lived in false righteousness; he had become respectable again. No debt was hanging over his head. He lost his own repentance, and forgot he had received forgiveness.

Application

You have no goodness outside of God's mercy. Besides forgiven sins, God's mercy has spared you from thousands more and greater. You are a beggar. You are respectable because God forgave you. Be grateful for God's forgiveness and you will never demand full payment from others.

"Should you not have dealt mercifully with your fellow servant, as I dealt with you? (V-33)

Thought

That's logical. No defense against that accusation. The contrast is too clear. The debt is compared to what was owed him. The man hadn't looked at things that way. He didn't see God's viewpoint until too late.

Application

Are you willing to ask the question "What does God think of me?" What's God's view of this matter? These questions might seem far away; too difficult to even get answered. If you never ask that question, you will see everything incorrectly. You have the wrong values, and the wrong goals. Your whole world will be upside down. First things will be last and last things first. So seek God's view of your decisions.

179

CHAPTER 54
SEXUALITY IN THE KINGDOM
(19:1-12)

Some Pharisees came up to him and said, to test him, "May a man divorce his wife for any reason whatever?" (V-3)

Thought

Two different rabbinical thoughts existed on this topic. The Pharisees were going "to test Him," to put Jesus in a corner; to get Him locked into theories. They would do anything to remove His power over peoples' hearts! Anything to remove His authority that came directly from the Father.

Application

Do you approach Jesus with your head or your heart? The head tries to grasp and control. The heart surrenders. Don't use your head against your heart. The head should be used after your surrender to Jesus. If you use your head so you don't have to surrender, you are a Pharisee!

"Have you not read that at the beginning the Creator made them male and female..." (V-4)

Thought

Once more Jesus breaks through the law, refusing to accept either rabbinical theory. He goes to the beginning and the Father's design for marriage. Jesus believes He can overcome all of history's sins and restore everything as at the beginning.

Application

Jesus can restore you, as "at the beginning." At your beginning, the Father had a design - just why He made you. Much has happened since then. In some ways you haven't always followed that design. Jesus knows He can restore you. Even if you have entered into divorce, the Father's design for you can be accomplished in Jesus.

Thus they are no longer two but one flesh. (V-6)

Thought

To be "one flesh" means totally one. Marriage isn't "part-time" nor a "partial committal." A person enters marriage from within, totally and completely. This relationship is unique, as Christ to His Church (Eph. 5:22-24) and the union is not in the couple's wills, but in the Father's plan.

Application

If you are married, reflect on your committal. Examine it in the light of being "one flesh." What harms that ideal? What breaks down the oneness? If you are single, seek the Lord's guidance. Discern relationships. With whom can you be "one-flesh" as the Father wants?

"...let no man separate what God has joined." (V-6)

Thought

These famous words, known by everyone, have been interpreted in many ways. Unfortunately many interpretations are attempts at robbing the words of meaning. Let's not destroy the words! They are a saving power in the midst of great confusion. They are a tower of light inviting us all out of the darkness. The words are not clever rabbinical teaching. They are simple words, bringing God's power.

Application

"What God has joined" puts the relationship in the sacred, the untouchable. The words aren't meant to condemn, but to release God's help. Read them again and let their power enter into your own marriage. They will cast aside confusion and help you to see the Father's desire. Your marriage partner is different than everyone else and your marital relationship is unique.

"Because of your stubbornness Moses let you divorce your wives." (V-8)

Thought

Suddenly, the law is no longer God's. The Pharisees felt they had a perfect objection, an appeal to Moses. But Jesus hasn't come from Moses, but from the Father. He doesn't bring Moses' message, but the Father's.

To some degree, people can understand Moses easier than the Father. The Father's words force people not to quit too early. Everything revealed by Jesus is a mystery. Mysteries can't be reduced to legal terms. They cannot even be comprehended, speaking more to the heart than the head.

Application

Take these words to heart. They are not cruel words. They are Jesus' words. His words always bring consolation and strength from the Father. Don't run away from these words. Don't cut them out of your bible or your heart. Pray over these words and let the father speak to you through them.

"...whoever divorces his wife (lewd conduct is a separate case) and marries another commits adultery..." (V-9)

Thought

The words in parenthesis are probably a pastoral exception introduced by the Church. For Catholics, the bible is sacred, the powerful word of God. But Catholics are not "trapped by the bible," for they have a living word in the official Church. Sometimes, what seems a marriage, is not really a "union in God." Let the Church decide that.

Application

You can be scandalized in two ways, - by the seeming "harshness" of Jesus' words or by the seeming kindness of the Church in thinking of exceptions, or even in entertaining the thought of adjudicating difficult pastoral cases. But the Church is Christ's "Kingdom already existing in mystery" (Vatican II) and helps you to live Jesus' words without becoming hopelessly entangled.

"Not everyone can accept this teaching, only those to whom it is given to do so." (V-11)

Thought

Jesus challenges us to a radical commitment, or beyond what anyone could expect. Like a master teacher, he sees more possibilities in His students than other instructors. Jesus doesn't water down. He doesn't get caught in the "least common denominator" mentality that breeds indifference. He calls to the heights.

Application

What call is within you? What words do you hear as you read these texts? Those words will come frequently. They will stir you; move and call you. Jesus' words stir. They move and inspire. Listen to them.

CHAPTER 55
DON'T WAIT - TODAY IS THE DAY
(19:13-22)

"Let the children come to me.
Do not hinder them." (V-14)

Thought

It's true that Jesus' teaching is for adults. The message demands a committal. The children wouldn't understand everything. However, they could still be changed. Original sin already had touched them. They, too, had to be freed. The world had already delivered them it's message of selfishness. They needed to meet Truth Himself.

Application

Many parts of your childhood need to be touched. Many forgotten influences are buried within. You have been twisted, bent, broken, forgotten, set aside. A moment with Jesus can change all that. No one hinders you from coming. No disciple stands in your way, blocking you. Come to Jesus.

And he laid his hands on their heads
before he left that place. (V-15)

Thought

Jesus regularly laid hands on adults. Here, He touches the children. Imagine the power in those hands, and the changes in the children. Sin was forgiven and evil powers had to leave. Bodies were healed and minds touched. "Before He left that place" means that Jesus didn't want to delay bestowing His gifts.

Application

The same power comes to you when you believe. The gospel is God's power in Jesus, symbolized by laying on

184

of hands. Let Jesus lay His hands upon you. Let it happen now. Don't leave this place until Jesus has touched you.

"Teacher, what good must I do to possess everlasting life?" (V-16)

Thought
Very few questions in the gospels are sincere. Most come from people trying to catch Jesus. This question, though, flows from a good heart, searching and seeking to be better. Everything is ready for the Kingdom's gift. This man is already going in the right direction, seeking everlasting life.

Application
What do you seek? What questions come spontaneously to mind? What thoughts preoccupy you? Who owns your heart? Do you seek things above or those of earth? Where is your treasure? Are you really interested in knowing what good you must do for life everlasting?

"If you wish to enter into life, keep the commandments." (V-17)

Thought
The commandments are the door. Jesus talks about free choices; deliberate decisions for good or evil. The commandments are clear. They shouldn't be changed or altered. They are life's gates.

Application
How do you keep the commandments? Start with the basic ones listed in V18-19. Be honest. Don't kid yourself. Face the basic responsibilities. Jesus, in asking you to keep the commandments, also offers you His help.

"I have kept all these; what do I need to do further?" (V-20)

Thought

The man's second question goes even deeper, revealing a good and ordered life, deliberately maintained to reach the Kingdom. Now, he wants to insure his entry. He sees the Kingdom's overriding importance. Nothing is going to keep him out. He awaits a further word. Up to this point he merits only praise.

Application

If your life is in order, then go further. Ask what more can be done. Look around for other good deeds. In your generosity doors will open. You will stumble upon something new. You will meet others who also seek the Kingdom. The commandments are the door to eternal life, but don't just stand at the door, go inside, you are safer there.

"If you seek perfection, go, sell your possessions and give to the poor." (V-21)

Thought

This is not Jesus' frequent or stock answer. Others were told to go home. Others were just told to be quiet. Zaccheus generously donated a fourth of all he owned, and that seemed enough. (But for this man, the test concerned all his possessions.) Jesus would never ask the impossible. This man was so generous that "selling all" was within his reach.

Application

Just what does God seek from you? You can't discover that by reading. Even reading the gospels is not enough. You need two gifts:
1.) To listen to God's word within.

186

*2.) To have a spiritual guide to discern with
you. Slowly God's answer will unfold and you
will find your call.*

Hearing these words, the young man went away sad, for his possessions were many. (V-22)

Thought

No one can say that the man lost out entirely on the
Kingdom. After all, he still kept the commandments.
But he let an opportunity slip. He will never realize all
that might have been. Today, we don't even know his
name.

Application

*Who are you? What does God call you to? How are
you spending your days? Don't let opportunities slip
by. Discovering God's plan for you is still ahead.*

CHAPTER 56
THE KINGDOM'S RICHES (19:23-30)

"I assure you, only with difficulty will a rich man enter into the kingdom of God." (V-23)

Thought

The Old Testament saw the rich as God's favorites and
their treasures as proof of God's love. Jesus sees riches
quite differently. They are attractions drawing the
person away from the Kingdom. The rich young man,
who just turned down Jesus' invitation, provides a clear
example.

Application

*Your heart cannot be divided. You, like everyone intent
on being a disciple, have to face the questions
surrounding material ownership. You have to provide*

for yourself and your family, yet not allow material goods to become a false kingdom. Be generous, especially to the poor, for that covers a multitude of sins.

"...it is easier for a camel to pass through a needle's eye than for a rich man to enter the kingdom of God." (V-24)

Thought
Jesus uses a common proverb with the two extremes of "Camel" and "needle's eye." He applies the saying to the question of the rich entering the Kingdom. It would be easy for people to pass over these words, thinking they apply only to the extremely rich. This teaching, however, is for all. Anyone can make material goods his kingdom. If "riches," no matter how small, are the person's kingdom, then he will have difficulty entering Jesus' Kingdom.

Application
Don't go around examining all your material goods, wondering which ones you should get rid of. Rather, give your heart to Christ's Kingdom and then gradually "let go." He will do His work in you. When others need some of your material goods, then give freely and the Kingdom will be yours.

"Then who can be saved?" (V-25)

Thought
Suddenly, the rich had gone from being God's favorites, certain to be saved, to hardly having any chance at all. The disciples, as on other occasions, couldn't understand this total turning around. Later they would understand that Jesus' Kingdom was not of this world and that the rich would be too attached to this world to choose the Kingdom.

188

Application

You can't learn about the Kingdom overnight. This understanding comes gradually, beginning within as you see the Kingdom's importance. The understanding grows as you give thought and time to the Kingdom. Eventually you see what you have to surrender. By then, you are willing.

"For man it is impossible; but for God all things are possible." (V-26)

Thought

Some would say that Jesus is "watering down" his "camel-needle's eye" statement; that the proverb was only a figure of speech, meant to draw attention to His teaching on riches. That's not true. The statement stands. No one, by his own power, can be detached enough for the Kingdom. The Kingdom has to be God's work in us.

Application

First you must want the Kingdom with all your heart. Secondly, you must realize that no matter what you do, you can't gain this treasure by yourself. Then, you have beginning wisdom. Your desire for the Kingdom will cause a helplessness that will bring you on your knees to the Father, who alone bestows the Kingdom.

"Here we have put everything aside to follow you. What can we expect from it?" (V-27)

Thought

"Everything" for the apostles meant some torn fishing nets. Yet, here they are with hands outstretched seeking a reward. Obviously, the Kingdom's power hadn't come to them yet. They had walked with Jesus, but the message hadn't penetrated. In so many ways they still did not understand.

Application

How many years have you attended church and even eaten of Jesus' Body and Blood? These years don't guarantee that you understand the Kingdom. That understanding comes from within. You have to be stirred. You have to see that Jesus' Kingdom is vast and powerful and beautiful. You have to want to be a member more than anything in the world. Then God's action can begin.

"...in the new age when the Son of Man takes his seat upon a throne befitting his glory,..." (V-28)

Thought

Everything seems to stay the same. Certainly, people are born and die; new homes are built and old buildings are torn down. But it's still earth; still 24 hours a day; 12 months a year; so many years to a lifetime. But it won't always be the same. Something new is coming, and has already begun in Jesus and all who follow Him.

Application

Don't be fooled. The present age that seems so permanent is passing away. Only Jesus' Kingdom will remain. Don't waste your life choosing the present age, giving your allegiance to what passes. You can give your life to the Kingdom, that has already begun in Jesus begins within you.

"...everyone who has given up home, brothers or sisters, father or mother, wife or children or property for my sake..." (V-29)

Thought

Jesus doesn't say anyone will actually lose all those possessions. Everyone's situation is different. Some will always have their parents, siblings or spouse.

However, moments will arise when the Kingdom demands that one or more of these is given up; allowed to go forth; not held on to. Jesus' words are a consolation. Those moments of human loss are touched by the Kingdom's consolations.

Application

The Kingdom will bring you freedom. You will not be grasped or choked by possessions. Everything you have comes from the Father. Be ready to return everything to Him for the Kingdom's sake.

CHAPTER 57
THE DISGRUNTLED WORKERS
(20:1-16)

"...the owner of an estate who went out at dawn to hire workmen for his vineyard." (V-1)

Thought

In this parable all receive an invitation and all respond. Some come earlier and some later. Each person has his own time to hear God's voice. No one determines when God speaks or invites. God is sovereign. His will is unfathomable.

Application

You cannot say "Please call me to the vineyard later" and you cannot question "Why did you not call me earlier in life?" God is speaking to you now. He calls you now. Listen and respond now.

"After reaching an agreement with them..." (V-2)

Thought

Our God even comes to terms with us. He who made us, sits down and bargains. He makes sure that we

191

understand our commitment and see our reward. He invites a freely given service with no arm twisting, cajoling, manipulating. He can't explain everything, since we haven't even seen the vineyard. But He seeks an enlightened commitment.

Application
Jesus wants you committed to His vineyard. Where, when and how are the daily questions. Ask for light on these questions. Your commitment is to a God of light who wants you to understand your call and accept your place in His vineyard.

"He came out about midmorning." (V-3)

Thought
God's vineyard is endless. There is always room for one more worker. In fact, the laborers are few. Many who are called don't respond. The owner is always searching the world's street for some who can help.

Application
God calls you. Even if you were not in the first group, He still calls. Even though some of your life has passed, you can still serve. Mid-morning is not the usual time to begin a day's work but God still calls you to the vineyard.

"You too go along to my vineyard and I will pay you whatever is fair." (V-4)

Thought
These workers have no strict right to a full day's pay. Some time has been frittered away, whether in "sowing wild oats" or in confusion about where to work. However, the owner generates trust. These men don't bargain ahead of time. He must seem fair to them. They are grateful to get work when the day could have been totally wasted.

192

Application

What feelings are inside you? Do you see time as slipping away and still you have not found your life's work? Have you walked a road which you thought was for you and then discovered otherwise? Have you wasted the early years and spent them foolishly? Let Jesus come. You can trust Him. He will be more than fair with you. When you accept His offer, you will be grateful that your whole life was not thrown away.

"Why have you been standing here idle all day?" (V-6)

Thought

The usual owner wouldn't be going out in later afternoon. Little work can be accomplished now. For the workers' part, there is little chance to be hired at this late hour. But, God is not the usual owner. He never stops. Never gives up. Never says, "That's enough." He always thinks, "There's room for more."

Application

Don't feel that it's too late for you to serve God. The world may have already retired you, or discarded you, or said you weren't useful. You may be limited, confined to a bed or a wheelchair, or laid up with an infirmity. God still wants you for the vineyard. To Him, no one has outlived his usefulness, for the vineyard is vast and needs everyone.

"...but begin with the last group and end with the first." (V-8)

Thought

The process seemed backward but the time sequence is important to the parable. Those who worked the longest would begin to feel justified in seeking more. If they were paid first, they would have gone home, not

193

knowing the owner's generosity. Instead they had to cope with the problem of all receiving equal pay.

Application

God understands time. He knows that certain events have to happen to you first. Then others will follow. You can feel that events should have happened differently. You might complain, "If only this had happened this way instead of that." Put these feelings aside. Trust the Owner.

"...you have put them on the same basis as us..." (V-12)

Thought

The men, in their complaints, seize upon the final group. Logically those hired at mid-morning, who received beyond the pay scale, could also complain about these one hour workers. According to everyone's logic, everyone has a right to complain. People see life according to their way of seeing things. That's not faith. Faith tries to see life according to God's logic.

Application

By this parable, Jesus invites you to be lifted above those feelings that gnaw away at you. Within you are complaints, hurts and feelings of mistreatment that no one else sees. Let them all pass. Be freed.

CHAPTER 58
TWO SONS AND TWO BLIND MEN
(20:17-34)

"But on the third day
he will be raised up." (V-19)

Thought
Every verb is passive as if Jesus surrenders into other's hands. He leaves His suffering and death to others. Even His resurrection is in His Father's power. He gives Himself into men's hands, because the Father wills that. When they will have finished, He then totally is in the Father's hands.

Application
Do you always want to take things into your own hands? Do you think that you must control your life and destiny? Jesus teaches you to surrender; to give your life over into the Father's hands. Don't you see that with each passing day your life slips away from you no matter how you hold on. Let the Father hold on to you, then you are safe.

"...one at your right hand and the
other at your left, in your kingdom." (V-21)

Thought
The mother unknowingly asks for the right gift - a place in heaven for her sons. However, she probably didn't understand the Kingdom. She saw the crowds and the earthly glory; the chance for success and power. She didn't understand.

Application
Often you ask Jesus for the wrong gift because you don't understand. You need light to understand the

Kingdom. You often seek things that would ruin the Kingdom within you. First you must see the Kingdom, then you will know what to seek.

The other ten, on hearing this, became indignant at the two brothers. (V-24)

Thought
None of them understood either. They heard the words "Kingdom of Heaven" but they still dreamed of an earthly kingdom. They hadn't yet been to Jerusalem. There, all their false illusions will be shattered by the cross and the true dream restored by the Resurrection.

Application
Realize how much the world's vision ensnares you with false visions and passing goals. Come up to Jerusalem now. There you will see the true picture - the fragileness of life, the power of evil and the final victory of the Kingdom.

"It cannot be like that with you." (V-26)

Thought
Jesus isn't satisfied with the world as it is, because human life shouldn't be this way. Every problem in this world is rooted in how people relate to one another. Unfortunately, selfishness dominates human relationships. Competition, manipulation and exploitation abound. Relationships in the Kingdom are quite different. When the Kingdom is present relationships aren't built on self-interest.

Application
Do you want to change the world? Then let Jesus' Kingdom come to you. As the Kingdom comes, you will change the way you relate to others. No more taking advantage; no more lying; no pushing others around;

196

no more seeking your own glory and power. In the Kingdom, you will serve the others.

Suddenly two blind men sitting by the roadside... (V-30)

Thought

Matthew contrasts the two apostles, who didn't see the true Kingdom, with two blind men, who did. Although they only "heard Jesus was passing by," they knew the Kingdom was at hand. This was their moment, their chance, their invitation. They took advantage. They didn't waste the moment or let it slip by.

Application

Every day, the Kingdom's moments come to you. Don't waste them or let them slip away. These moments will never come again. If you are faithful to these moments, you will grow sensitive to the Kingdom and will be attentive to even the slightest word from the Father.

"What do you want me to do for you?" (V-32)

Thought

In the previous story, Jesus asked the same question of the mother. However, He couldn't fulfill her request. She was asking from human motives and envisioned earthly glory. However, the blind men were seeking the Kingdom. They were asking at the Father's prompting.

Application

What stirs within you? Earthly desire or the Kingdom? Jesus wants you to ask, but your petitions must flow from the Kingdom. Seek first the Kingdom, and the other needs will be cared for too.

197

Immediately they could see; and they became his followers. (V-34)

Thought

What a gift! From blind men hopelessly confined to a wayside existence, to being followers of Jesus. Right up there with the sons of Zebedee!

Sometimes the Kingdom moves quickly and change is sudden, spontaneous and far-reaching, coming when least expected.

Application

Don't limit the Kingdom. Its power sweeps away mountains, restores bodies, gives sight, changes lives, and makes followers of Jesus. Whatever you need is yours. Just seek first the Kingdom.

CHAPTER 59
THE KING CLAIMS HIS CITY (21:1-11)

As they drew near Jerusalem, entering Bethlehem on the Mount of Olives. (V-1)

Thought

To the Jewish mind, the Mount of Olives evoked Messianic hopes. Later (24:3) Jesus will be seated on the Mount of Olives while describing His second coming.

For a while, the cruel death on the cross, so associated with Jerusalem, is overshadowed by the glory that will result.

Application

You share Jesus' glory by Baptism. Jesus is already your Messiah. Yet your full glory is still hidden,

198

revealed to you slowly, and often accompanied by
suffering. Do not allow yourself to be discouraged.
The sufferings of the present are not equal to the glory
to come. Keep your eye on the glorious crown
awaiting you.

"The Master needs them" (V-3)

Thought

Two lowly creatures are about to carry the Messiah into
his glory-filled Jerusalem. If animals could be in
heaven, these two would be the first. They were used
by Jesus for His glory. Just the words, "The master
needs them," released them from any other
commitment.

Application

The same mystery happens every day. Jesus needs you
to bring Him to others. Your words and deeds are the
two lowly animals bringing Jesus into His glory. Allow
yourself to be freed from other cares. When the Master
needs you, put everything else away quickly

This came about to fulfill what
was said through the prophet: (V-4)

Thought

The Father had prepared all of this for centuries. His
Messiah would not come unannounced. His glory was
planned even before the death on the cross.

Jesus did not disappoint. He didn't back down. His call
to glory included the cross and the mystery of death.

Application

The Father has planned your glory from the very
beginning. He rejoices in bestowing your glory. Jesus
delights in sharing His glory. Don't back down from

199

hardship. Persevere. Take courage. God's darkness is
only a little while. True life begins and ends in glory.

So the disciples went off and did what Jesus had ordered. (V-6)

Thought
Everything here is clear, Jesus describes their task clearly - even how to accomplish it. The time is right away. With that clarity, the disciples set out quickly and with joy.

Application
When God's will is clear, your task is easy. When that will is not clear, when darkness and confusion muddle the scene, then doing God's will and even knowing His will is extremely difficult.

Learn to discern. Grow sensitive within to God's promptings. Learn from past mistakes. Look at the results (the fruit good or bad) and store up wisdom for the future. Your task should become easier as you learn God's clear will for you.

The huge crowd spread their cloaks on the road. (V-8)

Thought
The crowd always has a sense of God's presence. They don't wait for a theological explanation. They even act against the wishes of the Sanhedrin. They know that the Father is acting in Jesus.

The crowd gives an unlimited welcome. Nothing is too much. Cloaks and cut branches adorn Jesus' path. They totally surrender to Him.

Application

Don't wait. Surrender now - totally, fully, completely. Hold nothing back. Place everything at Jesus' feet. This time is special. The Spirit's activity sweeps through the world and through your heart. The Kingdom is at hand! Let go. Stop clinging. Jesus alone is your security.

Those following kept crying out: "hosanna to the Son of David!" (V-9)

Thought

The highest acclaim they could find! Jesus shared David's prerogatives while entering David's city of Jerusalem.

The confrontation had now moved from the northern outskirts of Galilee to the political and religious center - Jerusalem.

Application

You are His city, His temple. He claims you as His own. His death bought you back, redeemed you from darkness and slavery.

How do you feel and think about Jesus Christ? Is He meaningless to you? Does He still seem to be on the outskirts, like Galilee? Or, has He come to you? Ask Him to come. Let Jesus possess you by His Davidic right, forming you into His new Jerusalem.

As he entered Jerusalem the whole city was stirred to its depths. (V-10)

Thought

This is the son of Mary, Joseph was just a carpenter. What has happened to this carpenter's son? Why is this powerful city "stirred to its depth?" Why do they ask

"Who is this?", when all know he comes from Nazareth.

Obviously, this stirring doesn't come from human birth or talents. The Son of David is here. The owner of Jerusalem has come to claim the city. It is the time of visitation.

Application
Let yourself be stirred. It's good to ask "Who is this Jesus?" Right now is a special time. Other answers haven't worked. Ask the real question. "Who is Jesus and where can I find Him?" You don't need to go anywhere. He comes to you. The time of your visitation has come.

CHAPTER 60
CLEANSING AND CURING (21:12-22)

Jesus entered the temple precincts and drove out all those engaged there in buying and selling. (V-12)

Thought
Jesus' Kingdom and evil cannot coexist. No peaceful compromise exists. The Kingdom claims everyone and everything, shaping all to the Father's glory.

Even the temple needs a cleansing. Nothing should belong more to the Father than the Jerusalem temple. If the very heart of David's city is impure, how can the Kingdom come?

Application
Let Jesus go to your heart, to your feelings, thoughts, goals and desires. These form your inner temple from which flows your actions and choices.

*No one wants to be cleansed there. Even so, let Jesus
enter. Stop covering over your hidden self. Stop living
only on life's surface.*

"Scripture has it, `My house shall be called a house of prayer.'" (V-13)

Thought

Don't miss Jesus' vision. He sees what life can be and
what the Father intended from the beginning. The
temple was built for man to praise God, and for people
to know the living God. Instead the money changers
have taken over, and men are stealing God's glory.
Jesus had to act.

Application

*Jesus has a vision of you. He knows what the Father
wants for you from the beginning. He sees your sins
and how you have stolen His glory. But it's not too
late. He hasn't turned from you. He hasn't given up.
He sees the goodness within and the person He can
make of you. Seek Jesus' cleansing action.*

The blind and the lame came to him inside the temple area and he cured them. (V-14)

Thought

What a different response! The blind and the lame use
the temple correctly. Those who need God's mercy,
who have no money to change, receive everything
freely. The Kingdom has come.

Here, Matthew records His final story of Jesus' healing.
No need for further signs. The hour of victory is at
hand.

Application

Jesus freely pours out His gifts. He welcomes the chance to restore sight and limbs. The teaching is clear. The Kingdom will restore you. God's gifts are plentiful. Let Jesus claim the temple that is His - your body and soul.

The chief priests and the scribes became indignant when they observed the wonders he worked. (V-15)

Thought

In Chapter two, Matthew also mentioned the chief priests and scribes. Jesus' life was threatened, as Herod was upset by the Magi's story. Their coming on the scene signals that Jesus' life is threatened again. No more skirting the issue. The highest powers in Israel are going to face the question of Jesus Christ.

Application

At times you run away from this question. You put off until tomorrow life's basic question. "Why did God make you?" "Who is Jesus?" Stop running from these questions. Let the Kingdom come!

"Do you hear what they are saying?" they asked him. Jesus said to them, "Of course I do!" (V-16)

Thought

No matter who proclaimed Jesus to them, the chief priests and scribes were not about to listen. Their minds were closed. Nothing could convince them. Even Jesus rising from the dead wouldn't change their minds. Were they blinded by intellectual pride or fearful of what others would say? They never seemed to examine their motives.

Application
What holds you back from the Kingdom? What questions and fears dominate within? Let them come forth. Don't turn away from Jesus. The Kingdom is so easily available. So many acclaim the Father's gift in Jesus. Deal honestly with your inner obstacles. Ask yourself why you don't yield to the Kingdom's invitation.

With that he left them. (V-18)

Thought
Matthew's symbolism is stark. Jesus is finished with the chief priests and scribes. They have had their chance. He had preached openly. The people and the children proclaimed Him, but they were closed and indignant.

Jesus will continue doing His Father's will, even if the religious leaders don't follow. The leaders, however, can't remain neutral. By their office they have to act on this question. Unfortunately, their decision destroys.

Application
You can't remain neutral. Jesus will either be our King, Lord, Savior and Redeemer, or He will be a constant nuisance, a perpetual reminder of your poor choices and your deliberate, selfish acts. No middle ground exists. No way to avoid the dilemma. Surrender to your King! Don't destroy yourself.

Seeing a fig tree by the roadside he went over to it, but found nothing there except leaves. (V-19)

Thought
God had provided everything for the tree yet there was no fruit to feed the people. The tree led an entirely selfish life. It didn't understand it's role in nature. It's life was supposed to help others to live.

Application

How much has God done for you? Why? For your well-being? Yes, but also for others. You are supposed to be life-giving, bringing forth life and supporting life. Your power, your bank account, your resources will be held against you on the day of judgment, unless you used them for life.

CHAPTER 61
THE DEEPER QUESTIONS (21:23-32)

"On what authority are you doing these things? Who has given you this power?" (V-23)

Thought

Jesus was asked those questions long before signs and wonders showed His authority and power came from the Father. No one had made Jesus a teacher. No one anointed Him a Rabbi. The gift was within from the beginning because He is God's only begotten Son.

Application

By baptism, you share that anointing. Your power and authority come from your personal anointing by the Spirit. No one can give or take away your power and authority. However, you can set it aside, refusing to believe in it and to use it. Then your talent is buried and the Kingdom isn't preached as it should be.

What was the origin of John's Baptism? (V-25)

Thought

Jesus keeps to the main issue. The central question is, "Where is the Kingdom?" Where is God active right now? These chief priests had to face their past discernment. They hadn't accepted John the Baptist. They were blind then and they are blind now. They didn't see God acting in John and they don't see Him acting in Jesus.

Application
Keep your heart on one question. Where is God acting now in your life? Don't turn from that question. Learn from past mistakes. At other times you received an invitation to the banquet and refused. At least see now that you should have accepted. Even if you have said "No" before, say "Yes" now to God's action in your life.

"Was it divine or merely human?" They thought to themselves. (V-25)

Thought
Since they refused the simple invitation to believe in Jesus (and John) they now have complications. God's invitation in John and Jesus was simple and straightforward. The denial is now twisted and complex. They are prisoners of their past choices. They cannot be set free. Even now, Jesus would gladly receive them. However, they can't set aside their past.

Application
Jesus invites you to the Kingdom. The invitation is simple. Yet, whenever you walk away from the Kingdom, life grows complicated. You no longer have a single goal, or an eternal promise. Without the Kingdom, your life shatters in to many pieces, becoming fragmented and broken.

"So their answer to Jesus was, "We do not know." (V-27)

Thought
The religious leaders cannot even answer this simple question about John the Baptist. The people had answered that question years ago. They had flocked to

John and were baptized by him. They became his disciples and followed his teachings.

But the people had nothing to lose. They had nothing to protect. They didn't have to keep a facade or pretend. They were free to see clearly where God was acting.

Application
Are you free to respond to God? To act according to His call? Have you experienced God's call within, and have not acted? What was the matter? What obstacles prevented your free response? When the Kingdom is present, you must be free to respond.

"What do you think of this case?" (V-28)

Thought
God respects man's unique power to think. He doesn't expect "blind obedience" with no rational foundation. Jesus doesn't try to bypass people's thoughts. He reaches deeper beneath the surface. He forces everyone by His parable to face the truly deep questions within.

Application
Everyone has these deep questions. They are ultimate questions of human existence. Why do I live? Is there a God? Who is Jesus? Is there life after death?

Don't cover over these questions. Don't let your daily cares and worries bury these questions. Let Jesus uncover your deepest searchings. Then you will see clearly the Kingdom's value.

The son replied, "I am on my way, sir"; but he never went. (V-29)

Thought

This was a surface reply. The son knew his father wanted this response. This answer avoided any confrontation, but it wasn't true. The words didn't come from the heart. The son never accepted the father's request. He just wanted to get out of the house. His reply was too quick. There was no time of conversion.

Application

If the Kingdom remains on the surface, as a superficial reality, then your words might sound good but your heart will be far from the Kingdom. You will always be professing what you don't live out. Instead let the Kingdom sink deeply into you. Then make your profession of faith.

This son said in reply, "No, I will not;" but afterward he regretted it and went. (V-30)

Thought

Why did he regret his reply? Many thoughts must have raced through his mind. Did he think of his father's past goodness? Of his own selfishness? Or of the good results when he finished his task?

Application

Think about the heavenly Father. These thoughts are the beginning of your life with God. As you raise your heart and mind to God, different thoughts will come. You will consider God's goodness; the shortness of life; your past choices; the many helps God gives; the special trials that show you need Him. Each thought has the power to change your direction.

209

CHAPTER 62
THE OWNER AND THE TENANTS
(21:33-46)

Listen to another parable. (V-33)

Thought
Jesus piles proof upon proof. His teaching comes together. The honest person would long ago have believed. Yet Jesus still tries to "get through," to "break into their lives."

"Listen" means that the words get deeper than the ears. They must pass to the heart, mind and will where the person determines his life's direction. This parable calls the listeners to walk a different path than the one ending in death.

Application
Just listen! Let this parable speak to you. The figures are clear. The meaning is so obvious that the parable has a special power.

"...a property owner who planted a vineyard, put a hedge around it, dug out a vat, and erected a tower." (V-33)

Thought
The owner is God. The hedge, vat and tower represent all that God has done. The rest of the parable portrays every person's basic decision, whether the creature will return the fruits to the Creator.

Application
Recognize the source of your existence. What do you have that you haven't received from God? You can't claim anything as totally yours. The real owner was working long before you existed.

"Then he leased it out to tenant farmers and went on a journey." (V-33)

Thought

God gives them free will. They had dominion over their goods, freely deciding how to use all the owner left them. The laborers seem to be industrious and the harvest is gathered. Here the problems begin. Selfishness destroys what God planned for man.

Application

Is anything missing in your life? You work hard. You produce the fruits of labor. Yet, is something not there?

Do you forget God's share? Do you claim everything as your own, as if you made the world? Do you share with God's poor? Do you share fairly with your family? What happens to the fruit of your labor.

"...he dispatched his slaves to the tenants to obtain his share of the grapes." (V-34)

Thought

The slaves came in the master's name. After all, the owner had planted and dug and put up the tower. However, the tenants wouldn't listen to that legitimate voice. They snuffed out the slaves, as if the owner would not try again.

Application

Within you is the voice of conscience. Each day that voice speaks clearly, reminding you of God's purpose. It calls you back and leads you away from rash decisions. Don't snuff that voice out.

The tenants responded by seizing the slaves. (V-35)

Thought
The slaves stood between the tenants and their selfish ambitions. It would have been better if they hadn't come. Now cheating the owner is more complicated. Anger had led to murder.

Application
Whenever you grow angry, God is trying to say something. Often you don't want to hear that word. Instead of just destroying the cause of your anger, reflect. Why have these words angered you? What's happening within you? What do you need to hear?

Finally he sent his son to them. (V-37)

Thought
The son is Jesus. The slaves are the other prophets sent previously to remind Israel of its debt to God. However, the tenants have already acted selfishly. They are too far down the road to turn back. Now they have to murder the son. They move quickly in that direction.

Application
Don't let sin gain power over you. If you allow a little selfishness to begin, the need for more will grow. Then you will be trapped and sin will prevail.

Instead, listen now to God's word. That word is within you by conscience, and outside of you by Matthew's words. This parable has power to turn you away from sin.

"What do you suppose the owner of the vineyard will do to those tenants when he comes?" (V-40)

Thought

After such a clear description, even the bystanders can answer. Jesus' wisdom has delineated Israel's history, putting His finger directly on the problem. The leaders never listened to the prophets.

Application

You should know how you stand with God. You should have a clear idea of whether you walk a true road or a false one. Do you stand right with God or does this parable apply to you? What kind of tenant are you?

CHAPTER 63
THE FATHER'S BANQUET (22:1-14)

Jesus began to address them, once more using parables. (V-1)

Thought

Again Jesus tries. He is like the owner going out even in late afternoon to gather workers. He doesn't use parables to confuse or cover-up a teaching. These parables are clear and powerful. The stories remain in people's hearts long after the telling.

Application

Let this parable remain in you, you need to hear over again the same truths. The parables say that the Kingdom is available in Jesus to all who are open to receive.

"...likened to a king who gave a wedding banquet for his son." (V-2)

Thought

The king has two desires. He wants to exalt his son and to share his joy with all. The king has known the son

213

from all eternity. He created human life so all could share in the Kingdom. Every person born into this world is invited to share the banquet.

Application
When God made you, He invited you to the Kingdom. You couldn't understand then, because you still had to hear the gospel. Now the invitation is clearer to you. You hold the invitation in your hands. You see it's importance. Don't turn it down.

"See, I have my dinner prepared! My bullocks and corn-fed cattle are killed; everything is ready."
(V-4)

Thought
This verse sums up all of Christianity. The Father has done everything for us. We just have to be interested enough to accept. It takes time to get interested in the banquet. (Because the world attracts and the Kingdom seems so far off.) The servant is told to describe the banquet, giving the person time to be attracted by the invitation.

Application
Compare the time you give to the world's attractions and the time you give to understand and find the Kingdom! A taste and a desire for the Kingdom come slowly. You have to set aside time. The Spirit has to work on your imagination and intellect. Let Him picture the Kingdom for you. Let your imagination "taste and see" the banquet. Then you will come.

Some ignored the invitation. (V-5)
The rest laid hold of his servants, insulted them, and killed them. (V-6)

214

Thought

Neither came to the banquet. The first group are indifferent people. The others are evil people. Neither was really interested in the Kingdom. Something else claimed their hearts. So the invitation is rejected.

Application

Today, you have an invitation to the Kingdom. The invitation is "everywhere and every moment." However, there is a secret. Don't be influenced by those who aren't interested. Seek out those who have found the Kingdom. These are the teachers and guides who invite others. By their words and deeds they will offer you an invitation.

"...go out into the byroads and invite to the wedding anyone you come upon." (V-9)

Thought

The chief priests and Pharisees criticized the people following Jesus. This parable turns the tables. Even though of lowly estate, the people at least heard the invitation. They had chosen the better part, even though they didn't get invited at first.

St. Paul asked - "Just who are the rich, the wise, the powerful and the famous?" Whoever accepts the Kingdom's invitation.

Application

What do you prize? Your talents, riches, human powers, or your state in life? They are the wrong goals to cherish.

Value only one gift. You have an invitation to the Kingdom. Sell that invitation for nothing the world offers. Treasure that invitation, putting it ahead of all else. Some day you will banquet with the King and His Son.

215

The servants then went out into the byroads and rounded up everyone they met, bad as well as good. (V-10)

Thought

There is not enough time to draw up a new list, or to see just who is who. The Kingdom had to be full. Some are people who served the King and others who didn't, "the bad as well as the good." What right do the bad have to eat with the king? At least they were interested enough to come.

Application

You will never understand God's thoughts. The Father so much wants this banquet. You will never understand the twists and turns of history. Why have some accepted and others rejected the Kingdom?

Understand just one thing. You are invited. How did you get on the list? There is no list anymore. In Jesus all are invited. The door is wide open. Preach that good news to everyone.

"...he caught sight of a man not properly dressed for a wedding feast." (V-11)

Thought

The invitation is for everyone. However, accepting the invitation implies a willingness to put on proper clothes. All, when so suddenly invited, were not properly dressed, but most grasped the need of some minimal preparation. Obviously, this man didn't feel the need to prepare.

Application

You can't enter the Kingdom as you are. Something must happen when you receive the invitation. Some effort to prepare. Don't affront the King. Take the invitation seriously and get ready for the banquet.

216

CHAPTER 64
QUESTIONING GROUPS (22:15-33)

"Then the Pharisees went off and began to plot how they might entrap Jesus in speech." (V-15)

Thought

This is useless, harmful activity, the very opposite demanded by the Kingdom. People shouldn't "go off" but "come closer" to Jesus. They shouldn't "plot how to entrap" but ask how they can receive Jesus.

Why do they act this way? They perceive the Kingdom as a threat instead of a gift.

Application

How do you perceive the Kingdom? As an intruder into your life? As something you wished "went away?" As something you don't want to think about? Let God change your ideas of His Kingdom. Don't run away, but remain still and pray, "thy Kingdom come."

They sent their disciples to him, accompanied by Herodian sympathizers. (V-16)

Thought

This is a strange mixture, since Pharisees and Herodians had two different views about Rome and the emperor. Evil joins them together in common plotting. Removing Jesus from the scene is a mutual interest.

Application

Are any of your relationships rooted in evil? Do you have friends who share evil with you?

Unfortunately, evil, when a shared interest, can bind people together. The Kingdom changes that. It removes evil from the heart and destroys relationships rooted in evil.

217

"You court no one's favor and do not act out of human respect." (V-16)

Thought

Although said to flatter, the sentence described Jesus. He was inwardly true, motivated by His love for the Father, bending to no one and following no human master. He was free. He was "His own man." The Kingdom penetrated His every thought, feeling and word.

Application

You, too, are called to that freedom. You should bow lowly to no one. You are owned only by the Father.

The Kingdom bestows freedom. It frees you from every other feeling of "being owned" or "being used." Jesus dreams of restoring you to the fullness of your human dignity by giving you the Kingdom.

Why are you trying to trip me up, you hypocrites?" (V-18)

Thought

Jesus didn't intend to offer them the Kingdom. No wisdom will be shared with them. They will not receive even the smallest opening to the Kingdom because they seek to ensnare rather than surrender themselves.

Application

All wisdom will be given to you. However, you must remove from your heart any desire to use the Kingdom for your own advantage. Don't ask God to bless your plans. Ask God to reveal His plans for you. Everything is stored up for you waiting to be released. Just come in good faith.

"Then give to Caesar what is Caesar's but give to God what is God's." (V-21)

Thought

They came to ensnare. They were hunters seeking to carry off Jesus in their nets. Instead they go away "empty handed," with nothing to show except embarrassment.

It is always that way with the selfish. Greed closes their hands and they can't receive God's gifts.

Application

How do you go through this day? Are you an "entrapping" person or a "giving away" person? Do you use people and situations to your advantage, or do you seek God's plan and His role for you? When you give everything away, your hands are prepared to receive the Kingdom.

"At the resurrection, whose wife will she be..." (V-28)

Thought

With this dumb question the Sadducees thought they proved there was no resurrection. To them, everything was logical. They had studied the law and had reasoned from it to definite conclusions. They were locked into their "wisdom" and locked out of the Kingdom.

Application

Don't let your thoughts, your reason, your logic and wisdom keep you out of the Kingdom. Many are blinded by their own thinking, not realizing that wisdom is a gift from above. The Kingdom invites you out of your own little world into God's world.

"You are badly misled because you fail to understand the Scriptures and the power of God." (V-29)

Thought

They were really off course. They didn't even share in normal Jewish wisdom about eternal life. How did they get this way? They had withdrawn from the faith community where God was acting. They were a "lone-ranger" group, feeling they didn't need others.

Application

God gives you the Church to interpret Matthew's gospel and every word of Scripture. This interpretation doesn't limit you. It helps you to grasp.

God doesn't call you to walk the Scriptural path alone. You, too, can become "badly misled." He gives you a Church and a faith community with established teachers and guides. Listen to them.

CHAPTER 65
WRONG WAY TO THE KINGDOM (23:1-12)

"But do not follow their example." (V-3)

Thought

Jesus clearly denounces the Scribes and Pharisees. Matthew uses them as figures of those who have not lived up to the Kingdom. Clearly then, people can be "in the Church" and yet not "in the Kingdom." They can be accepted by everyone and yet be far from God's plan.

Application

Where are you "with the Kingdom?" Do you honestly seek God within? Or do other gods dominate your

*thoughts and feelings?   Even though you might
externally seem "religious," are you truly seeking the
Kingdom?   Let Jesus' words free you from religious
illusions that might ensnare you.*

"Their words are bold
but their deeds are few." (V-3)

Thought
A person gets deceived by his own words. Speaking
frequently about God can cause religious illusion.
Truth rests in deeds, the concrete results of faith. Talk
is often a smoke screen, fooling especially the speaker.

Application
*Don't examine your words about God.   Examine
instead your deeds. Examine the hidden, selfless deeds
that others can't praise.   Examine the deeds you
accomplish in hiding.   Do the truth in secret,
performing deeds known only to the Father.*

"They bind up heavy loads...while they themselves
will not lift a finger to budge them." (V-4)

Thought
Rigorism runs rampant. That's bad enough. What is
worse, they bind others to their rigorism while excusing
themselves.

Jesus is different. He frees people from bondage. He
accepts others' burdens. Contrast the "heavy loads"
placed on man's shoulder, with "my yoke is easy and
my burden light."

Application
*Don't make religion a strongman's game of heavy
burdens. True religion means receiving the Kingdom.
Your burden is to seek the Kingdom; to tell all about*

221

the Kingdom; and to accept the inevitable suffering entailed in bringing about the Kingdom. This is a far cry from senseless rigorism.

"They are fond of places of honor at banquets and the front seats in synagogues..." (V-6)

Thought
Taking places of honor isn't the same as entering the Kingdom. The "front seats in synagogues" are "man-given honors." The Kingdom is reserved for the "the little ones" by the Father. These human honors bring about religious illusions.

Application
Don't be fooled by the world, nor by its honors. The Kingdom comes quietly. It comes within. The Kingdom is God's inner word that leads you to serve other people, not to seek their praise.

"One among you is your teacher, the rest are learners." (V-8)

Thought
The Scribes and Pharisees kept looking at human teachers. They took pride in being an important teacher's disciples. Yet their teaching was hollow, based on human respect, human applause and vainglory. They were looking the wrong way, and missed the real truths, revealed freely to the little ones.

Application
Where do you seek your wisdom? From the latest survey? Studies? From the latest worldly news? From your own brilliant thoughts?

Jesus alone is your teacher. No one else can give you the wisdom you need. His wisdom shows you that only the Kingdom perdures.

222

"Only one is your father, the One in heaven." (V-9)

Thought

Jesus had received everything from His Father. He taught that His Father was everyone's Father. All can know the Father. They can experience the Father and seek every gift from Him.

Application

"Only one is your Father..." seems like a cold statement, cutting away the warmth of human fatherhood. You have to understand. All human fatherhood is but a shadow, a sharing and participation. Don't stop with your earthly father, go also to your heavenly Father, "from whom every family in heaven and on earth takes its name." (Eph. 31-15)

"The greatest among you will be the one who serves the rest." (V-11)

Thought

Jesus sums up His teaching in one sentence. From now on ambition, self-serving and glory-seeking will be seen clearly as part of the world. They aren't part of the Kingdom.

Application

Where can you serve? Who needs your talents and gifts? Who would be served by your charity? You are called to service. Hidden in that call is your kingdom-gift. Search for your place and moment of service. Ask God to reveal how He calls you to serve.

CHAPTER 66
WOE TO YOU! (23:13-24)

"Woe to you Scribes and Pharisees..." (V-13)

Thought

This hard phrase shows Jesus' impatience. He knows the Kingdom is at hand. He knows that all should enter. However, the Scribes and Pharisees are neither entering nor admitting "those who would."

Application

This day Jesus invites you to enter the Kingdom. Your invitation is everywhere, in the feelings in your heart, in the thoughts in your mind, in this gospel of Matthew, in the events of the day. Everywhere, in every situation, the Father says "Come into the Kingdom."

"You travel over sea and land to make a single convert." (V-15)

Thought

They certainly had zeal. They sought to bring about their kingdom. However, their Kingdom isn't the same as Jesus'. They have a confused kingdom where people don't learn that God is Father. Before being so zealous they should understand the Kingdom. Then they should "travel by sea and land."

Application

What are your feelings and thoughts about the Kingdom? Do you see God as Father? Do you understand that He always cares; that He tries to help; that every day He provides for you? Before anything else happens, let Jesus give you a correct and true idea of His Father's Kingdom.

224

"...but once he is converted you make a devil of him twice as wicked as yourselves." (V-15)

Thought

Jesus didn't like the results of their "conversions." The converts got turned into the wrong direction. This is Jesus' general complaint. Later, He will be more specific. He doesn't like what He sees. He knows the true Kingdom and realizes that these converts aren't experiencing the life He has with the Father.

Application

With the Kingdom, comes changes. They should be good changes, as you experience the Father as Jesus does. Conversion should make you more patient and less judgmental; more forgiving and less critical. The Kingdom includes laughter, friendship, enjoying the Father's creation, better relationships and a total well being.

"If a man swears by the temple it means nothing, but if he swears by the gold of the temple he is obligated." (V-16)

Thought

The statement doesn't make sense. That's what Jesus is complaining about. The Scribes and Pharisees have lost common sense and direction. They are "off the road," unable to reach the Kingdom themselves and leading others astray with them.

Application

It is easy to lose your way. That's why Jesus gave you the Church, with it's teachings, and the local parish with it's Eucharist. He also will provide other helps, such as good friends, a faith-filled spouse and Christian parents. It's important for you to judge correctly. Who in your life brings you closer to the Kingdom and who leads you away?

"The man who swears by heaven is swearing by God's throne..." (V-22)

Thought

The Scribes and Pharisees avoid basic responsibilities by clever formulas. Jesus says that no one will be saved or condemned by knowing or not knowing religious formulas. Salvation rests upon central issues. Is the person serving God? Is he faithful to the call in his heart? Is he seeking the truth. These are the central questions, not those of correct religious formulas.

Application

Jesus will never trick you. Your place in the Kingdom won't be decided by obscure religious truths or subtle theologies. The questions are basic. Each day you are invited into the Kingdom. Do you realize you have this invitation? Do you accept the invitation? Are you willing to live this day according to God's will? These are the clear, central questions you must answer.

"You pay tithes on mint and herbs and seeds while neglecting the weightier matters of the law..." (V-23)

Thought

All Jews owed religious tithes on food products. However "mint, herbs and seeds" are so small that even trying to figure out the tithes on these was ridiculous. While doing the calculating, the Scribes and Pharisees neglected important matters. They neglected justice and mercy.

Application

In your concern for the Kingdom, look at the important questions. Do you surrender your life to God? Is Jesus first in your thoughts and desires? Are you generous or does selfishness predominate? Concerning others; do you forgive? Do you seek the good of others? Do you manipulate people to your goals? These are the central questions.

"...swallow the camel!" (V-24)

Thought
These two words sum up the whole mess. What would these blind guides have to do to see? First, they would have to surrender everything they cherished; everything they had worked at for years. They would have to admit that they were blind and were leading people astray. Then they would have to seek out Jesus, the light of the world. In so many ways, they would have to begin over again. Obviously, these needed changes aren't easy, but Jesus didn't come to condemn but to save.

Application
Possibly you see parts of your life that have to change. Maybe that "part" is large. It might even be your whole life, even the total picture. Don't be discouraged. Be willing. Don't hold onto your blindness. Don't keep going the wrong way. Let the Kingdom change you, even if it means beginning over again in a whole new direction.

CHAPTER 67
WHITEWASHED HYPOCRISY (23:25-39)

"You cleanse the outside of cup and dish, and leave the inside filled with loot and lust." (V-25)

Thought

Jesus uses this example for the basic theme of His Kingdom. The true and powerful cleansing occurs within the person, not outside. Jesus is not content with external changes that leave the true problems untouched.

Application

Let the Kingdom's power go deeply inside you. Be quiet. Reflect. Let your mind be touched frequently this day by the Spirit. Otherwise the Kingdom will be superficial, touching only the outside of your cup and dish.

"You are like white-washed tombs..." (V-27)

Thought

Jesus couldn't have found a more powerful example. Since contact with tombs brought a ritual impurity, burial places were painted white as a warning. However, within the tomb was the total filth connected with dead bones. This figure is the perfect image, summing up Jesus' complaints against Jewish religious practices.

Application

Realize that sin has marred you; has misdirected and ruined your original goodness. Jesus doesn't call you to total self-scrutiny. He doesn't demand that you get yourself together. He only asks that you seek His Kingdom. The Kingdom itself will change you as you allow its power to get deeper than surface whitewashing.

"...while hypocrisy and evil fill you within." (V-28)

Thought

On the stage, actors don costumes and play a role. They even enter deeply into the character. But everything remains on the surface. The actor, in real life, doesn't change. While on the stage he pretends for a while.

Application

Don't be afraid of this demand. You shouldn't want to be the same as you were before the Kingdom came. These changes will free you. They are true results, the first fruits of God's presence. They prepare you for the Kingdom's full coming.

"You say, `had we lived in our forefathers' time we would not have joined them in shedding the prophets' blood.'" (V-30)

Thought

In many parables Jesus contrasted the forefathers' actions in killing God's servants and the present generation that would kill His Son. These parables were not listened to. The Jews continued to blame former ages for their sins, while overlooking what they themselves intended to do. Jesus doesn't let them get away with the deception.

Application

The world deceives you. Even friends flatter you. Few tell you the truth that can really help. Jesus' Kingdom lives only in truth. Seek the truth. Ask for God's light. Don't enjoy the darkness, it will ruin you. Full life comes with God's true word.

"Some you will kill and crucify, others you will flog in your synagogues and hunt down from city to city." (V-34)

Thought

These predictions, by the time Matthew wrote, had already been fulfilled. People who hated Jesus' words, hated also those who followed that word.

However, these words consoled the persecuted. Jesus foretold they would suffer. They would see His words come true, before their eyes and in their lives.

So God's word always draws a response. It is expelled and cast out by those who refuse to listen. It is grasped and cherished by the believers.

Application

How do you relate to God's word? Do you fear to hear that word, casting it out of your Heart? Does the word mean nothing, unimportant as far as you are concerned? Or do you seek, cherish and take deeply into your heart God's word?

"O Jerusalem, Jerusalem, murderess of prophets and stoner of those who were sent to you!" (V-37)

Thought

Quite a title. Jesus would want it written on the city gates, reminding everyone of a sad past. Even in modern Jerusalem the fighting continues, as if shedding blood were her destiny. How did the chosen city come to this? Step by step, it walked away from its destiny.

Application

Today, and every day, you will take some steps. In which direction? Quo Vadis? Away from your call and from your destiny? Or toward the Kingdom and

230

your glory? In all your years, you have only one day of decision - today!

"How often have I yearned to gather your children..." (V-37)

Thought

We know Jerusalem's story. Did the story have to be that way? If Jesus were to die, could He not have been accepted by His own, and then rejected by outsiders? Man is free. None of God's stories are inevitable. Jesus yearned for a different ending.

Application

Face your freedom. Jesus would gather you under His wing. Nothing is inevitable. No one has to be away from Jesus or alienated from the Kingdom. Even Jerusalem didn't have to crucify Him. It could have freely turned away from that deed. So turn away from everything destructive. Drop your anger and hostility. Come into His Kingdom.

CHAPTER 68
THE DISCIPLES' QUESTION (24:1-14)

His disciples came up and pointed out to him the buildings of the temple area. (V-1)

Thought

Obviously these buildings present an imposing sight. They are large and carefully sculptured. The gospel doesn't provide the disciples' words, but evidently they are in awe.

Application

The buildings represent everything that can overwhelm you. They represent the world's power, your problems, your distant goals, your inner fears, your powerful

231

anxieties, your deeply rooted guilt or past sins. This
chapter will put everything in perspective.

"Do you see all these buildings? I assure you, not one stone will be left on an other..." (V-2)

Thought
The imposing buildings are not really that powerful. Their destruction will be soon and complete. There will be "not one stone" and "all be torn down." Jesus knows what true power is. He has all power from the Father.

Application
Seek a correct relationship to the Father. Slowly, His power will tear down in you whatever opposes His will. You, however, will not be destroyed.

"Tell us, when will all this occur? What will be the sign of your coming and the end of the world?" (V-3)

Thought
Often the disciples asked questions that were out of order. This question, however, opens up a lengthy discourse, filled with warnings and predictions. Something has happened to the disciples. They have begun, at least, to ask good questions.

Application
God's grace often comes through a question that burns within you. The question flows from your heart and feelings. Let the question come. Ask the question of God. Listen for the answer. If the question is a poor one, God's answer will not make much of it. If the question is deep and true, then God's response will open an important door for you.

"Be on guard! Let no one mislead you." (V-4)

Thought

People are often faithful for years and then end up going off the track. What happened? Where did they go wrong? Wrong ideas entered their heads and got control. They became ensnared, more by their own understanding, than by the Kingdom.

Application

You can never take your eyes off the road. You can never presume to know exactly God's will. The Father reveals His will, day by day, to the little ones. Each day, ask not only for your daily bread, but to see where the Kingdom comes for you.

"`I am the Messiah!' they will claim, and they will deceive many." (V-5)

Thought

This "Messiah claiming" has occurred often in Jewish history. A people seeking and expecting a Messiah are open to deception. They follow foolishly in their gullibility. Although not totally responsible, they still suffer from their poor decision.

Application

Good will doesn't suffice. Seeking the Kingdom demands wisdom and prudence. Test the Spirits. Discern your inner promptings. Seek out a competent guide. Gather friends who seek the Kingdom in truth. There is no need to go astray. Listen to the Church and be guided by your priests.

"You will hear of wars and rumors of wars. Do not be alarmed. Such things are bound to happen, but that is not yet the end." (V-6)

Thought

People jump to conclusions with wars and war rumors. They conclude that all the world's history is ending. Great foolishness follows belief in the worlds' imminent end. Even balanced people get caught up. Jesus says the world still has many generations. We must live, not only for ourselves, but for the millions who will come after us.

Application

Let the Kingdom bring you life. Let the Kingdom bring you inner peace that begets hope in struggles and dreams for the future. Pass on life. Don't live by rumors or doomsday talk. God has put life on this earth, and that life won't cease until He decides.

"This good news of the Kingdom will be proclaimed throughout the world as a witness..." (V-14)

Thought

This seems like a very vain and proud boast, considering that Jesus had but a few disciples who soon would disperse under criticism. Yet, Jesus knew from the Father that His "good news" was for all the world. That He would not see the gospel spread in His mortal life wasn't important. He knew the Father's will and promise.

Application

In your lifetime, you might see your grandchildren or even your great grandchildren. However, many generations will still be hidden from your eyes. Even now, you don't see all the good that comes from your words and example. Sow the Kingdom's seeds, until the day when your hands become lifeless.

CHAPTER 69
THE FINAL COMING (24:15-35)

"If a man is on the roof terrace, he must not come down to get anything out of his house." (V-17)

Thought

In Israel, the stairs from the roof to the ground were outside the house. Going inside would be an unnecessary delay. Jesus asks, *in normal times*, that the Kingdom come first with no delays or excuses. Certainly when the prophetic word is actually happening, no time remains for any delay.

Application

Don't put off the Kingdom. Don't say "tomorrow" when Scripture always says "today;" not "later" when Jesus says "now." Don't delay your good works. Don't delay your decisions taken in prayer. Don't put off your good intentions until tomorrow. Today is the Kingdom's day. Tomorrow is uncertain.

"...for those days will be more filled with anguish than any from the beginning of the world..." (V-21)

Thought

This is a great mystery. These difficult days will affect the good and the bad; those responsible for the evil and those totally innocent. Jesus seems able only to warn, to predict and to give some direction. He, Himself, seems helpless to totally change or turn away these days of suffering.

Application

God's mind holds so many mysteries that even His revealing them, brings only more questions. Don't let yourself be carried away with speculation. Don't even ask "Why is this happening to me?" Answering that

235

might bring only more questions. Choose the Kingdom.
Work to relieve sufferings in others. Then believe and
trust. That is all you can do.

"For the sake of the chosen, however, the days will be shortened." (V-22)

Thought
God will treat the elect like a loving father giving
medicine to a child. God sees how much the child can
accept. He then stops, knowing the child can take no
more. The travail of these days is due to hidden and
buried sinfulness; to powers that are not understood
even with Revelation and Scripture. These evil powers
are over you, stronger than you. Our only protection is
the Kingdom.

Application
You might or might not live through the days described
here. Even in so called "normal times," evil is still over
you; stronger than you; able to crush, destroy, ruin and
pillage everything you are and have. You don't know
what "days" lie ahead. You do know they will be
shortened for those who have chosen the Kingdom.

"...so if they tell you, `Look, he is in the desert,' do not go out there;..." (V-26)

Thought
In disasters, all are adversely affected. Some make
things worse by poor choices in reacting. Others size
up the situation, saving themselves and others. Besides
shortening the days for the elect, Jesus also gives some
advice, so problems aren't multiplied.

Application
Don't multiply your problems. Don't apply ineffective
remedies that make matters worse. Don't overreact,

trying to straighten everything out with some extraordinary action. If you are among the elect, you won't get fooled. You will know that the Kingdom doesn't save you from every human suffering. You will keep your peace and seek God's way of bringing the problem to a conclusion.

"...the sun will be darkened, the moon will not shed her light, the stars will fall from the sky..." (V-29)

Thought

The Jews believed that these heavenly bodies were angelic forces that controlled human history. These forces will lose their power before Jesus claims all history as His own. Symbolically, they represent the "false idols" that control people. One by one the beauty of fashionable living, the grandeur of riches, the strength of powerful corporations or of nations will fall. Standing alone in His beauty and grandeur and power will be Jesus.

Application

This "falling from the heavens" happens every day. Riches are lost and power passes to another. So, choose Jesus as your Lord. Forsake the riches. Don't be deceived by false powers. Jesus alone remains, the true Lord of all history and joy of the elect.

"...and all the clans of the earth will mourn..." (V-30)

Thought

"The clans" mean unbelievers. They will "strike their breasts" for they have had no share with Jesus. They have set His Kingdom aside for other choices. The elect, however, will rejoice. Their faith and waiting have come to an end. They rush to meet Jesus, whom they have always treasured in their hearts.

237

Application

Sounds like a fairy tale, yet nothing is more true. Life quickly passes and only Jesus remains. So choose the Kingdom now. Choose totally, firmly, once and for all. Don't put off the choice. The Kingdom is at hand. The sun, moon and stars will pass. Only Jesus remains, together with the elect who awaited Him.

"...they will assemble his chosen from the four winds..." (V-31)

Thought

Jesus isn't a celebrity who wants applause from admirers. He knows His elect. He sends for them and gathers them. What a beautiful gift, - to have an angel come with the message that Jesus wants to see them. For most people that message comes at death's hour, when they slip quietly into His hands. For a few, the message will come at the world's end. Just when, doesn't matter.

Application

To have Jesus send for you. To have Him send an angel. To hear such a beautiful message, "Jesus wants you to be in His house this day." The reward of a lifetime. The final gift of the Kingdom. To be with Jesus. It is yours. Believe and choose and remain faithful.

CHAPTER 70
THE MASTER'S COMING (24:36-51)

"As for the exact day or hour, no one knows it neither the angels in heaven nor the Son,..." (V-36)

Thought

Since the Kingdom is the Father's banquet for the Son, everything is kept a surprise. The final and full gift of all history will be given to Jesus when the Father decides. People can't enter the Kingdom by some secret knowledge of when it's coming. Some make the mistake of claiming the Kingdom's coming too early (previous parables). Others grow disheartened at its delay. The Kingdom demands the difficult attitude of waiting, watching and preparing in faith.

Application

Be clear about the Kingdom's demands. You must wait until an unknown time; watch even though you don't know when the Master comes; expect His coming and don't turn to other matters. Those demands are more than you can live up to. The Kingdom has to come to you as a gift, bringing a special attraction that consoles you during this unknown waiting period.

In the days before the flood people were eating and drinking, marrying and being married. (V-38)

Thought

Certainly nothing is wrong with eating, drinking and marrying, the very essential acts of human society. The condemnation comes because, besides these, the people didn't prepare for the Kingdom's coming. Eating, drinking and marrying were all they did, leaving no room for waiting, watching and expecting.

Application

Do you have room today for the Kingdom? Amid your hurried activity; your coming and going; your eating and drinking; where is your watching and expecting? Is there any turning of your heart to God? Or any moments of thanksgiving? Or even times when you ask that the Kingdom come?

Two men will be out in the field; one will be taken and one will be left." (V-40)

Thought

"Taken" means into the Kingdom. "Left" means "for destruction." The examples show that no social group is excluded from the Kingdom nor guaranteed entrance. The external social position is really indifferent. Being "taken" requires the interior dispositions preached by Jesus.

Application

Right where you are now, in whatever social or economic class, ask to be "taken." Ask to be among the Kingdom's members. "Being taken" comes at any time and any place. These are moments when God invites you to new life in Jesus. This reading prepares you for those moments. Ask now to be included in those "taken."

"Stay awake, therefore! You cannot know the day your Lord is coming." (V-42)

Thought

It's difficult to stay awake and to keep on watch. It's so easy to fall asleep or to turn to other pursuits. Yet, why does human life exist? To pass a few years here on earth? Or is man meant to be lifted up to a new life, a different world, the banquet prepared by the Father?

Application

Let the Kingdom be real for you. That's the only way you will stay awake. Let the Lord's coming be engraved in your heart. That's the only way you will watch and pray. Your life will quickly pass. The Lord comes soon. You cannot know just when, so you must stay awake.

"...if the owner of the house knew when the thief was coming he would keep a watchful eye..." (V-43)

Thought

It's easy to watch, when the exact time is known. All the resources are pulled together for that short period when the thief comes. Jesus asks the extraordinary. He asks us to live with that same intense watchfulness every day. A difficult demand! But the Kingdom is worth everything.

Application

How well do you watch? Some days you are fervent. Other days slip by with little watchfulness. What's the secret? How can you watch every day? When the Kingdom claims your heart and when you see the Kingdom as the only absolute, then you will watch faithfully.

"Happy that servant whom his master discovers at work on his return!" (V-46)

Thought

"Discovers" shows the servant had no idea the master was even around. It means the work was done every day as part of the normal routine of fidelity to the master's tasks. "Happy" because the servant is rewarded.

Application

Don't be fooled. You can't "plan" when the Master will "discover" you. Be faithful today to His tasks, even though you think His coming is far off.

Keep your heart on the "happiness" that awaits a faithful servant. You can't imagine the joy of hearing Jesus say "Come into My Kingdom, forever and ever."

"But if the servant is worthless and tells himself, `My master is a long time in coming,'..." (V-48)

Thought

This is the Kingdom's biggest problem. People feel the Master's coming is so far away. He delays. Life seems so long. Why not just eat and drink? Tomorrow is time enough to wait and watch. Tomorrow is not the day of salvation. Tomorrow is not the time to watch. The Master is not far away. The Kingdom is at hand.

Application

Open your eyes. The Kingdom is everywhere. The Master comes to you today. In every situation and every event, He comes. He is near. Don't be fooled. Don't say that He delays, when really He constantly returns. Rejoice that He is near. Then you will be a faithful servant.

CHAPTER 71
THE BRIDEGROOM'S COMING
(25:1-13)

"The reign of God can be likened to ten bridesmaids who took their torches and..." (V-1)

Thought

Jesus continues the familiar examples, stressing that although people are grouped together (bridesmaids waiting for the groom) and might seem the same, they really vary. The important difference has to do with the Kingdom.

Application

Accepting the Kingdom doesn't mean widescale, external changes. God doesn't intend to move you out to a desert or a monastery. You will continue life as before. The changes are within. Your goals will be different. You will seek and hope now for Jesus, the bridegroom.

"The foolish ones, in taking their torches, brought no oil along..." (V-3)

Thought

Providing the torch with oil demanded a complete desire to greet the bridegroom. Forgetting the oil could easily be excused. Besides, he would probably come during the day. Meeting the bridegroom didn't totally occupy the foolish. The sensible ones took no chances.

Application

If your desires for the Kingdom are true, then give yourself completely to the preparations. Be caught up in His coming. Let this expectation completely dominate your thoughts. Anything left undone in seeking God's Kingdom is foolishness.

"The groom delayed his coming..." (V-5)

Thought

The foolish are never prepared for a coming at the wrong times. That's why they are foolish. They don't see the Kingdom's importance. The sensible rejoice and are prepared, no mater what time the Kingdom comes. That is all they seek.

Application

Don't let anything interfere this day with the Kingdom's coming. You must give your time and thoughts to many matters, but keep your heart for the Kingdom. Never be too busy, too occupied or too engrossed. Don't miss Jesus when He comes.

"At midnight someone shouted, `The groom is here!'..." (V-6)

Thought

In the night's very middle! No one is awake. The perfectly wrong time for the bridegroom! Who can be expected to be ready at midnight? Yet that is the test. Someone seeking the Kingdom is always ready. Even in sleep, their hearts are on God. Even in night's middle, they still seek first the Kingdom.

Application

Your entering the Kingdom can't depend on external circumstances. Don't assume that it's convenient, not too difficult, or relatively easy. True, sometimes the Kingdom will be that way. At other times, it will be midnight. Your entrance depends on your internal dispositions that aren't overcome by external darkness.

"Give us some of your oil. Our torches are going out." (V-8)

Thought

They thought that they could always borrow the oil from someone. They were mistaken. Other people can help, teach or guide, but only God provides each person with the needed inner gifts (the lamp's oil). The external religious helps don't magically sanctify. The person has to allow his heart to be changed.

Application

You can be changed only if you put the Kingdom first. If your heart is elsewhere, then God cannot provide you with the needed oil of inner change. You have to choose. Do you give your heart to the world or to the Kingdom?

"No, there may not be enough for you and us..." (V-9)

Thought

Jesus tells us to share everything with the poor, but no one can share His Kingdom gift. That is too personal. The loving Father won't permit anyone to share that. No reason to share. The gift is abundant for all who seek the Kingdom.

Application

Cling to your gift. Cherish your portion of the Kingdom. Realize how personal that gift is. It is for you alone. It is the reason the Father created you. It is your part in Jesus' Body and your reception of His Spirit.

"While they went off to buy it the groom arrived." (V-10)

Thought

The Kingdom can't be put off. Certain tasks must be accomplished today. Certain preparations must be

245

made for His coming. Tomorrow has other duties. All must be complete before the groom comes.

Application
What are your Kingdom tasks today? Who should you forgive? Whom should you visit? You have duties of your state in life. Children to be cared for. Spouse to be loved. Every little task prepares for the Kingdom.

CHAPTER 72
SHARING RESPONSIBILITY (25:14-30)

"The case of a man who was going on a journey is similar." (V-14)

Thought
This parable represents the present state of the Church, since Jesus is now ascended to the Father. The Kingdom's money is given over to the disciples. Jesus' absence presents an opportunity for the disciples to exercise the master's authority and power.

Application
The Kingdom is in your hands. You aren't just someone who waits. You have gifts, a commission and command. You must bring the Kingdom to others. Your own entry depends on that.

"Immediately the man who received the five thousand went to invest it and made another five." (V-16)

Thought
Jesus gives here a fuller picture. Seeking the Kingdom doesn't just mean the passive waiting of the bridesmaids. Activity is involved. Intelligent planning is important. "And made another five" represents converts to the Kingdom.

Application

The Kingdom you received as a gift, give freely to others. You heard the news of the Kingdom from others. Let others hear the news from you. As the seed of God's word brings forth a harvest within you, scatter your seed on the fruitful ground. Others will reap. That's the Kingdom's way of growing.

"The man who received the thousand went off instead and dug a hole in the ground,..." (V-18)

Thought

Seeds buried in the ground bring forth a harvest. Buried money brings nothing. Even buried in a bank, money brings some return. In the ground it's totally inactive, wrongly placed and useless.

Application

Where do you place your gifts? At the world's service or God's? Do you bury the Kingdom, placing it hidden away? Bring forth your gifts. Place your time and energy at the Kingdom's service.

After a long absence, the master of those servants came home. (V-19)

Thought

Serving the Kingdom is not a matter of days, or weeks or even a few short years. The master returned "after a long absence." Some used the delay to think he was not returning. Others used the time well, to yield an even greater harvest.

Application

How much time do you have until the Master returns? That's unknown to you. How will you use this time? That's within your hands. So don't worry about "how long." Be anxious only to use well the gifts you have received.

247

"Come, share your master's joy!" (V-21)

Thought

Sharing Jesus' care for His Kingdom, should result also in sharing His rewards. "Joy" always means the banquet which the Father prepared for the Son. The tasks are over now. The work is complete. It's time for the banquet.

Application

Someday, your Master will return. All the cares and responsibilities will be over. The children raised. The marriage vows fulfilled. The religious profession lived up to. When your tasks seem difficult and overwhelming, realize they are only for a time. The banquet will soon begin.

"... so out of fear I went off and buried your thousand silver pieces in the ground." (V-25)

Thought

The first two dreamed of what they could do for their master. They rejoiced that he trusted them and shared responsibility. The third was paralyzed by fear. What if he failed? What if he lost the money? He so misunderstood the master.

Application

Don't let fear surround the Kingdom. Don't be paralyzed by wrong feelings about God. Nothing will be held against you. Perfect work isn't required. The harvest needs many laborers, each doing what they can. Do your best and you will rejoice at the master's return.

"All the more reason to deposit my money with the bankers." (V-27)

Thought

This wasn't an extravagant demand. The master didn't ask too much. Depositing the money required no genius, nor extra work. It represented the least possible effort. Seemingly, the master would have been satisfied with that.

Application

You might see yourself of little use to the Kingdom. Can't you at least deposit your gift to gain interest? You might not even know how to invest. At least you can search out where you can be of help. Get together with others who could know how to correctly use your talents.

CHAPTER 73
THE LEAST OF MY BRETHREN
(25:31-46)

"When the Son of Man comes in his glory..." (V-31)

Thought

That day will inevitably come. This is not doomsday gloom but Christian hope. All know the world will end. Scientists can show that inevitability. Weapons of ultimate destruction are already in place. The end, however, is not in mankind's hands. Jesus will decide when and how the end will come.

Application

Be wise. Realize your world and your life will end. Don't foolishly believe that you will escape the end. Prepare for His coming. The parable's details tell you how.

"Inherit the kingdom prepared for you from the creation of the world." (V-34)

Thought
The Kingdom is owed to no one. It's an inheritance given by a blessing. No one can claim any inherent right. No one takes the Kingdom by his own powers. The Kingdom is a universal gift, meant for all.

Application
It's meant for you. You are a co-heir with Jesus. You're named in the Father's will. You weren't just a recent addition, a last minute entry. Your name was there "from the creation of the world." Long before you even heard of the Kingdom, you were an heir.

"Then the just will ask him: `Lord, when did we see you hungry and feed you or see you thirsty and give you drink?'" (V-37)

Thought
Even the just are surprised. They acted so much in faith, that even they saw only darkly. They didn't fully understand. They didn't have the Kingdom's full light. They remained free to withhold their mercy. Those very elements are the source of the reward.

Application
If you were overpowered with light, if you saw clearly, there would be no reward. It's when the situation seems so human; when the person seeking help seems so selfish; when what you offer seems so little, that you are in the Kingdom.

"I assure you, as often as you did it for one of my least brothers, you did it for me." (V-40)

Thought

To serve the powerful is easy. To help those who might return the favor (or even greater ones) requires no faith. But to help those who will never be able to return the gift; to help the outcast, the alien, the despised, the poor, those seen as nothing in the world's eyes, requires faith. Poor and despised and cast out will soon be where Jesus is on Golgotha. He is still there. That's the only place to find Him.

Application

Don't miss your chances to help the poor. Jesus is there. Help those the world casts out. Jesus is there. Don't ask people to be respectable to gain your help. Jesus is hidden in every poor and rejected person. The world doesn't grasp this. Only those in the Kingdom can see.

"Out of my sight, you condemned, into that everlasting fire prepared for the devil and his angels!" (V-41)

Thought

A rather definite sentence. No parole involved. No time off for good behavior. The time for good behavior is over. The opportunities were set aside. The poor and the hungry were the door to the Kingdom, but they were turned away.

Application

You need the poor and the hungry. They are your invitation to the Kingdom. It's as simple as that. It's clearly explained. Care for them and you will be welcomed. Reject them and you will be set aside.

"Lord when did we see you hungry or thirsty or away from home or naked or ill or in prison..." (V-44)

Thought
The judgment seems so unfair to them. They are victims of some misunderstanding. They, supposedly, never had a chance. Others might have neglected the Lord, but certainly they didn't. He never came by. They never had a choice! Yet, He was all around them. He was there everyday, all the time. They never grasped how Jesus is one with those in need.

Application
The world is filled with hungry and poor and suffering people. So don't ask, "Where can I find the Kingdom?" Open your eyes. The doors to the Kingdom are everywhere. The Kingdom is as abundant as the needy upon earth.

"I assure you, as often as you neglected to do it to one of these least ones, you neglected to do it to me." (V-45)

Thought
This condemnation doesn't flow from one act. The neglect went on all the time. The sentence is more than fair. Day after day, year after year, the least ones were neglected. The heart wasn't open. The ears were deaf. The neglect was malignant, a cancer that ate away the person's inner being.

Application
Be aware of your neglect for the poor. Don't go on, day after day, year after year with "business as usual." That's not the Kingdom. The Kingdom changes you. You can't be the same anymore, once the Kingdom has come. The Kingdom moves you to activity. You will seek out the Christ. You already know where He can be found. He is where the poor, the destitute, and the rejected live.

252

CHAPTER 74
THE KINGDOM'S HOUR (26:1-19)

"You know that in two days' time it will be Passover, and that the Son of Man is to be handed over to be crucified." (V-2)

Thought

Matthew's gospel is filled with teaching. These last three chapters constitute the fifth part of his discourses. However, as these chapters unfold, Jesus speaks less and suffers more. He comes to the end of His teaching about the Kingdom, because the Kingdom itself is about to come.

Application

A time comes for you to stop hearing about the Kingdom and let God's power come. Throughout this gospel, Jesus has given you a clear invitation. The Kingdom is now at hand. Let it come! Don't just hear about the Kingdom. Welcome it! Yield to it!

At that time the chief priests and elders... (V-3)

Thought

The Kingdom's invitation was clear to them but they were accepting nothing. They chose their Kingdom over God's. After all, they already owned, possessed and understood their Kingdom. They didn't know what Jesus' Kingdom held in store for them.

Application

This is also your basic choice. Do you cling to your own kingdom; what you know, see, understand and have now? Or do you trust Jesus; surrendering what you have for His Kingdom at hand?

A woman carrying a jar of costly perfume came up to him at table and began to pour it on his head. (V-7)

Thought

This anointing of the head was reserved for the king. The woman, then, had two spiritual powers. She realized Jesus' importance by faith and she surrendered the entire jar by generosity. The act was full and complete, a sealing for His passion. Nothing was held back by either the woman or Jesus.

Application

You will gain the Kingdom by the same two powers. You must see by faith how important is Jesus' Kingdom and then surrender all you have for its sake. You can't be half in and half out. Give completely to receive completely.

When the disciples saw this they grew indignant. (V-8)

Thought

They didn't see. Jesus had just told them the Kingdom was only two days away. They still didn't grasp the urgency. They were still thinking of tomorrow, as if they had all the time in the world. Only the woman grasped that the Kingdom's hour was at hand.

Application

Whom are you like, the woman or the disciples? Do you say "Plenty of time yet, no need to hurry?" Or do you understand, after all these pages, that the Kingdom comes right now? There is never a tomorrow with the Kingdom.

"Why do you criticize the woman?..." (V-10)

Thought

Everything gets twisted. The woman who grasped the situation correctly is criticized by those, who themselves couldn't see. But Jesus, the Truth, straightens everything out. The woman of faith is praised and the unseeing disciples are silenced.

Application

Within you are different feelings and thoughts. Often they war against each other. You don't know how to respond. Be quiet and still, like the woman. She waited until Jesus spoke. She knew she had acted rightly and had not been foolish in her generosity.

"...wherever the good news is proclaimed, throughout the world what she did will be spoken of as her memorial." (V-13)

Thought

The woman is more than vindicated. She is lifted up to lasting, world-wide proclamation. That doesn't change anything. She wasn't turned aside by possible criticism. She won't be fooled by world-wide acclaim.

Application

These are the two problems, criticism and fame. Both can rob you of the Kingdom, unless you understand that only Jesus really matters. Only the Kingdom lasts. Only the good deeds done in selflessness endure. Everything else passes away.

Judas Iscariot went off to the chief priests (V-14)

Thought

From now on, everybody begins to manifest his true colors. It's the showdown. The time for talking is over.

The Kingdom's hour comes. The moment of truth uncovers what is within Judas. No commitment. Nothing untouchable. Everything for sale. The inside is quite different from the outside. It had always been that way. He had never accepted the Kingdom.

Application
What is within you? What is really deep? In the decision's hour, which way will you go? Really, the same way you have always gone. If you sincerely choose the Kingdom now, if the Kingdom now comes before everything else, you will also choose the Kingdom at your final hour.

CHAPTER 75
THE COVENANT MEAL (26:20-35)

When it grew dark he reclined at table with the Twelve. (V-20)

Thought
The Passover had to be eaten at night, because God's liberation from Egypt began at night. "Growing dark" symbolizes the end of Jesus' mortal life and the gathering power of the kingdom of darkness. In the approaching darkness, Jesus seeks the security of a meal with the Twelve.

Application
What do you do in the times of your darkness? What will you do as your earthly days come to a close? Seek out Jesus. He invites you to recline and eat with Him. Seek out the Eucharist. Seek out those who share the Kingdom with you. When your darkness comes, the heavenly Father offers you some security. Take advantage of His gifts.

"The Son of Man is departing, as Scripture says of him, but woe to that man by whom the Son of Man is betrayed." (V-24)

Thought

A religious problem exists here. Since Scripture prophesies that Jesus would be betrayed, then it had to happen. But how about the free will of the betrayer? Is he caught, like a Greek tragedy, doomed from the very beginning?

God, knowing what Judas would freely do, is different from God forcing Judas to act as he did. The latter didn't happen. The deeper mystery, which always remains, is why God allows us to freely reject the Kingdom.

Application

Your freedom is everywhere. With each free decision, you choose a direction. Even if you have chosen wrongly, you cannot eternally place yourself outside the Kingdom while you still live. You can't permanently runaway from the Kingdom on this earth. No matter how often you have freely chosen to reject the Kingdom, Jesus still invites you.

"Take this and eat it," he said, "this is my body." (V-26)

Thought

With these words, Jesus invited the disciples to share in the Kingdom - its glories and its sufferings. Having been with Him for these years, they are now asked for a commitment. They don't understand everything but they do know enough to say "yes" or "no."

Application

How long have you been with Jesus? During these years, He has shown you His Kingdom, and explained the demands and the rewards. He asks you now for a commitment. By choosing to eat His Body, you choose to share His Kingdom.

"All of you must drink from it," he said, "for this is my blood, the blood of the covenant,..." (V-28)

Thought
The Kingdom has a price, the blood of new birth. The American Indians believed that blood contained the person's life. They drank the martyr's blood to gain their courage. Jesus' new life is not just the transmission of new human life. It is the Kingdom's life, for all born into this world.

Application
How often do you receive the Eucharist? How do you receive? Routinely? Forgetfully? Mechanically? From now on, realize the Eucharist brings the New Covenant, the Kingdom of Jesus.

"I tell you, I will not drink this fruit of the vine from now until the day when I drink it new with you in my Father's reign." (V-29)

Thought
So much happens between these two drinkings! Jesus experiences His own suffering, death and resurrection. The disciples experience martyrdom. The Father's reign was still so far away. Yet Jesus saw it already existing. By His hope, he already possessed the Father's reign.

Application
So many obstacles! So many trials between you and the Father's reign! Enter into Jesus' hope. He already sees you with Him. He has your place prepared and

your name written on His palm. He provides every help. Nothing can keep you from the Father's reign.

"Tonight your faith in me will be shaken." (V-31)

Thought
One moment Jesus has them already with the Father. In the next breath, he says they will be scattered. He has no illusions. They are not perfect disciples. Even after the Covenant meal, they will fail. But their hearts are right. He will build on that.

Application
Don't get overwhelmed with the Kingdom's demands. Don't turn back, thinking that you can never be a perfect disciple. Your faith will be shaken. You will scatter in fame and failure, but do you come back? Do you allow the Kingdom to restore you or do you allow the shame of failure to win out?

"But, after I am raised up, I will go to Galilee ahead of you." (V-32)

Thought
Notice here. The flock is gathered again by the power of the Resurrection. Jesus, being "raised up," *is the Kingdom.* That has happened. The Kingdom has come. The Kingdom is everywhere and every moment from now until we meet Jesus.

Application
You don't enter into the Kingdom. You let the Kingdom enter into you. You can't pull yourself together and choose the Kingdom. Jesus chooses you. The Kingdom pulls you together. So don't worry and don't trust your own powers. Allow the Kingdom's powers full reign.

CHAPTER 76
SLEEPING AND FLEEING (26:36-56)

"My heart is nearly broken with sorrow." (V-38)

Thought

The warfare is at hand. The quiet years of Nazareth are far behind. Even the crowds, the healings and the miracles seem distant. Before, Jesus could speak calmly of His passion, because it was in the future. Now the sufferings are at hand. No crowds, no healings, only three disciples. Jesus is ready because He has always done the Father's will.

Application

The hour of trial, of suffering and passion will come to you. Don't worry about those future ills. When the time comes, you will be ready. Today is what matters. Be faithful this day and you will be faithful then.

When he returned to his disciples, he found them asleep. (V-40)

Thought

To sleep means, in Scripture, to be unaware of a critical time: to miss the grace; to be blind; to fail to grasp. With that the Kingdom is lost. What could have been, is not. They didn't have to sleep. They could have remained alert. It would have meant a lot to Jesus at that hour.

Application

Don't fall asleep. Don't miss today's grace. Don't fail to see and hear the Kingdom. It's important to Jesus. He wants to change you today and give you His spirit, right now. So stay awake. The time is critical. It's not just another day. It's time for the Kingdom!

260

"My Father, if this cannot pass me by without my drinking it, your will be done!" (V-42)

Thought

Jesus can't say "Our Father" because they are asleep again. He will walk the path alone, for He alone the faithful One of Yahweh. For Jesus, the Spirit overcomes nature. In Him, the Kingdom fully triumphs. Because of Jesus, the Kingdom can triumph in us, too, and even in the three disciples who fell asleep.

Application

Jesus' victory in the garden is your victory. Everything Jesus has He shares with you. He won the Kingdom for you. He was faithful and true to the Father, for you. Jesus' glory is yours. Don't miss the opportunity. Jesus' Kingdom is at hand.

"Sleep on now. Enjoy your rest! The hour is on us when the Son of Man is to be handed over to the power of evil men." (V-45)

Thought

Needless to say "sleeping and enjoying our rest" are out of place at this "hour." The power of evil has coalesced, bringing together Judas, Jews and Roman soldiers. Evil gathers it's forces from every side, soon to include even the people. Jesus stands alone. His troops are asleep and the faithful women aren't yet on the scene.

Application

Don't you try to stand alone. No need for that! You have the Father, Jesus, the Holy Spirit, the angels and the saints. You have those who share your journey on earth. Stay in their presence and don't let evil catch you being alone.

His betrayer had arranged to give them a signal, saying "The man I shall embrace is the one; take hold of him." (V-48)

Thought

Betrayed by an embrace - the ultimate contradiction! But then Judas had never been truthful. He had never surrendered to the Kingdom. He had always kept his own will, holding on to his own life and choosing his own way. The exact opposite of the Kingdom preached by Jesus. Not yielding to the Kingdom, he ended up betraying it.

Application

You can't be neutral about the Kingdom. You can't say, "Well, it's just there for those who want that type of life." You either choose the Kingdom or you betray it. You live either for Jesus or for yourself. You either waste your life on this world or spend it for the Kingdom.

"From day to day I sat teaching in the temple precincts, yet you never arrested me." (V-55)

Thought

Jesus will yield to their power, but first He makes them face what they are doing. He doesn't accept their arrest as logical or just. Was anyone in this armed crowd touched by His words? Possibly someone grew ashamed over getting involved in arresting Jesus. Hopefully, Jesus' words led to repentance.

Application

Jesus' words never condemn. They never lock you into guilt or shame. Jesus' words are doors. They lead to the Kingdom. Possibly someone found the Kingdom the very moment he came to arrest the King. You can find the Kingdom anywhere, at any time, even the moment of your most disgraceful sin.

262

Then all the disciples deserted him and fled. (V-46)

Thought

Until after the Resurrection, they will never be gathered again with Jesus. Seemingly, they had lost their last chance. No wonder they were so despairing when He died! They had fled. They had deserted Him. But Jesus hadn't left them. He came back to them.

Application

Jesus always comes back. He comes back to you. If you have fled Him, deserted Him, forgotten Him, denied Him, He still comes back. On the day you accept Him, He stays and abides with you. That's the Kingdom.

CHAPTER 77
TRUE AND FALSE WITNESSES
(26: 57-75)

Peter kept following him at a distance as far as the high priest's residence. (V-58)

Thought

This seems like a loyal action. How does it get Peter into trouble? Peter was confused and shaken. His following Jesus wasn't because of faith but from curiosity, guilt, despair and anxiety. He would have done better to return to Gethsemane and pray for an hour, as Jesus had asked.

Application

Be still within. Don't act from confusion or anxiety. When these fill your heart, stop and seek the Kingdom. Act only when God's light comes. In this way, your decisions will be in truth.

The chief priests, with the whole Sanhedrin, were busy trying to obtain false testimony against Jesus so that they might put him to death. (V-59)

Thought

They seemed to be acting backwards. The evidence should come first and then the conclusion. But their minds were closed. Jesus had to die. They had decided this. They will fit the evidence to their already formed convictions.

Application

Are you open to truth? Or, do you have many pre-conceived conclusions that certain people just don't love you; that others never give you a fair chance; that you have only limited gifts; that God hasn't been fair to you? You must let the Kingdom change everything, especially the prejudgments within you.

"This man has declared, "I can destroy God's sanctuary and rebuild it in three days." (V-61)

Thought

The teaching is an old one. Jesus explained already what He meant. They weren't interested then. Now, however, they can use the words for their advantage. They can condemn Jesus by His own teachings.

Application

Be still before God's word. Don't twist God's teachings to your selfish interest. Don't put Jesus' words aside, as if they held little importance. Don't use the word of God to condemn others. Use His words as your guide into the Kingdom.

But Jesus remained silent. (V-63)

Thought

For years he had taught openly and they hadn't listened. Words now are useless. They have chosen to reject the Kingdom. His words would only increase their guilt. In His mercy, He is silent. The Kingdom for them is now out of the question. It is hard to believe that anyone would reject the Kingdom, but they have reached that point slowly, but deliberately step by step.

Application

You never want to reach that point, so don't begin moving in that direction. Don't compromise. Don't put off the Kingdom until tomorrow. Don't turn a deaf ear to Jesus' words. The ultimate destruction comes when Jesus no longer speaks.

"Soon you will see the Son of Man seated at the right hand of the Power and coming on the clouds of heaven." (V-64)

Thought

Who is this Jesus? What does He bring? Who can claim to "Come on the clouds of heaven," unless He is God himself? Jesus certainly believes He is God. His resurrection will make the claim real. If that is true, then all should acclaim Him as Lord.

Application

Let the words flow from your lips, "Jesus, I acclaim you as my Lord, and I seek your Kingdom." It is a simple prayer. It opens you to the Kingdom. Say the prayer again; and let His Kingdom come upon you.

"He has blasphemed! What further need have we of witnesses." (V-65)

265

Thought

The witnesses are shams to begin with. They were needed only to fulfill the law. Later, other witnesses will arise who will proclaim to all the world that Jesus is Lord. These witnesses are true. They are needed so everyone can enter the Kingdom.

Application

You have heard these witnesses' story of the gospel of Jesus. You needed these witnesses to believe. Now that you have accepted Jesus and His Kingdom, be yourself a witness to others. Tell everyone of the Kingdom.

Just then a cock began to crow and Peter remembered the prediction Jesus had made. (V-75)

Thought

When Jesus spoke the prophecy, Peter didn't believe it. The words made him angry. He sought to talk Jesus out of His prediction. But Jesus wouldn't change His words. He knew they would soon bring repentance to Peter.

Application

You will frequently read Jesus' words. At the time you won't see the meaning. Later, however, they will come to mind, always bringing some gift. But if you do not read the gospels, Jesus' words are limited. They cannot be brought to your mind. So, read Jesus' words every day.

CHAPTER 78
PURCHASING A FIELD (7:1-10)

They bound him and led him away to be handed over to the procurator Pilate. (V-2)

Thought

This handing over was deliberate. Long ago conceived, carefully planned and now a "formal action." Their hearts didn't belong to the Kingdom. Evil owned them. Gradually they abandoned what was fair and just.

Application

Jesus appeals to your will, your intellect, your ability to choose and decide. He constantly offers you the Kingdom. He lets you experience and rejoice in the Kingdom. He entices you, warns you and teaches you. He fights for your heart. He so much wants to be your King.

Then, Judas, who had handed him over, seeing that Jesus had been condemned, began to regret his action deeply. (V-3)

Thought

This deep regret wasn't a true conversion, just anger and despair at the way everything turned out. His own ideas had failed him. He had lived by his own cunning and trusted in his own plans. All was now shattered.

Possibly, Judas was the most intelligent of the apostles. He certainly grasped the inevitable clash between Jesus and the Jewish authorities. He saw the problems clearly, but he trusted too much in his own intelligence.

Application

Learn this lesson well. Your God-given talent can be an obstacle to the Kingdom. That talent might be your

267

clever intellect or your power of analysis, or your brilliant thought process. Left alone, those powers will take you away from the Kingdom.

They retorted, "What is that to us? It is your affair!" (V-4)

Thought
The world so differs from the Kingdom. The world seeks its own advantage and gladly enters into self serving relationships. When the person no longer serves, he is then cast aside for another. The individual's problems mean nothing to the world. Money, profit and power are the world's goals. To personal problems the world says, "that is your affair."

Application
The world is wonderful to you when you are on top. But who cares for you when you are helpless and powerless, no longer of use? Jesus doesn't treat you that way. He seeks out the lost. He wants the powerless and sorrowing. He loves you when you are strong and when you are weak. He welcomes you even after your greatest mistakes. So whom shall you love and serve, the world or Jesus?

He went off and hanged himself. (V-5)

Thought
It didn't have to end this way. But no one was on the scene to help and Judas had cut himself off from Jesus. He is a symbol of tragic endings. It is the daily story, repeated thousands of times all over the world. Yet no life has to end this way.

Application
Look around. Who needs your help? Who are despairing, tortured, lonely? Who have cut themselves

268

off from others? Don't wait for them to ask. Extend a helping hand. Find time for them. Build bridges to their loneliness. You might help avoid a tragic end that needn't happen.

"It is not right to deposit this in the temple treasury since it is blood money." (V-6)

Thought
Now they start worrying about what is not right! They are more scrupulous about the money than about the life it sold away. Jesus had said that they swallow the camel, after removing the gnat.

Application
Don't get lost in unimportant questions. Jesus wants you to see the central questions. Are you fair? Forgiving? Truthful? Do you bring forth life? Do you offer hope? Where are your thoughts, desires and goals? Jesus asks "Where are you going?"

They used it to buy the potter's field as a cemetery for foreigners. (V-7)

Thought
Jesus always welcomed the stranger, the foreigner. He dreamed of a Kingdom which has no human distinctions of Jews or Greeks, male or female. All would be one in His Spirit. We were all foreigners, but now are heirs to an eternal home, paid for by Jesus' blood.

Application
Enter into this mystery. Set aside human divisions. In your midst are foreigners, people with different skin and strange language.

269

Even in your own household, you might feel estranged from spouse and children.   Only Jesus' Spirit can bridge those human differences.

They paid it out for the potter's field. (V-10)

Thought

The silver bought a field.   Jesus' blood bought a Kingdom. A few took advantage of this Potter's field. The Kingdom is for all. We are a purchased people, paid for and owned by Jesus.

Application

Accept what you are. You are a slave ransomed back; a child and heir of the Kingdom. The price has already been paid. The Kingdom is a gift. Faith opens you to its treasure. Fidelity to Jesus makes sure your bag has no holes.

CHAPTER 79
THE WORLD OR THE KINGDOM
(27:11-31)

"Are you the king of the Jews?" (V-11)

Thought

Jesus claimed to be Messiah.   However, the chief priests changed the title to "King of the Jews." Now Pilate could grasp the legal question. Pilate could understand "King."   That meant worldly power and armies and political allegiance. Obviously, that wasn't what Jesus preached.

Application

As you correctly understand the Kingdom, you will leave many worldly categories behind. You will move away from the world's solutions to problems. You will see a new life and a new way of relating with people. You will begin to see the Kingdom that Jesus has described.

He did not answer him on a single count,... (V-14)

Thought
It's too late for Jesus to explain now. A person doesn't grasp the Kingdom overnight. There is no "crash course." The Kingdom comes slowly. First, the seed of truth has to be taken to heart. Then the seed grows by fidelity to Jesus' words. Finally, the harvest comes.

Application
You must hear Jesus' word today. The Kingdom, like the harvest, doesn't come overnight. It comes gradually, in stages. Let Jesus do His work in you today, preparing you for His work tomorrow.

"Which one do you wish me to release for you, Barabbas or Jesus the so-called Messiah?" (V-17)

Thought
The choice is between the sinless Jesus and the notorious prisoner! But at this point, the chief priests wanted Jesus dead. The cost of the choice didn't matter. Jesus had to die.

Application
Don't think that Jesus' Kingdom costs too much. See what price the world exacts, with no return. The Kingdom's price is low.

"Do not interfere in the case of that holy man. I had a dream about him today which has greatly upset me." (V-19)

Thought

Even now the Father acts. He offers, through this dream intervention, a final chance for Jesus to be saved from death. Pilate, like Judas, remained free. The dream offers him a chance for the Kingdom. He is torn in so many ways. He faces Jewish leaders and unruly crowds. Now his wife's dream pulls him in a different direction. He decides to go ahead. It could have been otherwise.

Application

Today, both good and evil will pull at you. The Kingdom will come in many ways. The Father will intervene to save you. Evil will be powerful, but will not overwhelm you. The Kingdom's saving action will reach into the strangest places at the most unpredictable times. But you must choose. God's helps are invitations which must be accepted.

"Then what am I to do with Jesus, the so-called Messiah?" "Crucify him!" they all cried. (V-22)

Thought

The Jewish leaders have only one conclusion left. Having chosen their own kingdom, they have to get rid of the other Kingdom. Jesus said that a person could not serve two masters. He would love one and hate the other. Choosing the world, inevitably leads to rejecting the Kingdom.

Application

Be clear early on. You can't have both Kingdoms. One squeezes out the other and puts it to flight. You can't seek Jesus' Kingdom and still cherish worldly praise and honor. Otherwise, you are a house divided. Set aside your worldly ambitions, and seek Jesus' Kingdom wholeheartedly.

He called for water and washed his hands. (V-24)

Thought

Pilate condemns Jesus to death while calling Him a "Just man." He washes his hands, as if that absolves him of responsibility. He forgets that every human being is responsible. No one can say, "I am not human. I didn't have to choose." We are all human. We all have to choose.

Application

Each day you choose. You choose how to use your time, your gifts, your money. Because you are redeemed, you are free to choose the Kingdom. You have something worth living for. Your days have purpose, for the Kingdom is at hand.

Then they began to mock him by dropping to their knees before him, saying, "All hail, king of the Jews!" (V-29)

Thought

The words were right. They were able to bring salvation, if said from the heart. Instead, mockery abounds. It travels from one to another, drawing the whole cohort into its power. What soldier was free not to go along? They are all caught up in a Kingdom of evil they don't understand. They mock Jesus, who alone offers them freedom.

Application

Be aware of the powers that sweep you along. They are communicated to you by others. Those subtle pressures rob you of freedom by demanding conformity. If you resist and seek instead Jesus' Kingdom, you will receive that power from on high that will set you free.

CHAPTER 80
TAUNTING AND JEERING (27:32-44)

...this man they pressed into service to carry the cross. (V-32)

Thought

For Simon, the day had begun as usual. Then, he joined the crowd. Suddenly he is "pressed into service." The Kingdom is seemingly forced upon him. Later, when he understands, he will accept the gift willingly.

Application

Look at your own religious gift. It was probably given without your free will, the result of family involvement. That's a beginning. The time must come when you, yourself, seek and desire the Kingdom.

...they gave him a drink of wine flavored with gall, which he tasted but refused to drink. (V-34)

Thought

The wine would dull the passion and possibly be misunderstood years later. Jesus wanted to confront evil in its fullness, seeking no human comfort. He preached total dependence on the Father. He will not compromise at this point, when He has come so far.

Application

How far have you come? Maybe further than you think. Each day you try. Each morning you turn your face to the Father. Don't stop now. With the Kingdom, your efforts need be only a little while longer.

When they had crucified him, they divided his clothes among them by casting lots;... (V-35)

Thought

The soldiers sought the wrong gift. Jesus wanted to share His glory and power. They sought instead His clothes. They chose wrongly because they had no faith. They could see only Jesus' clothes and not His Kingdom.

Application

What do you see today? Can you see the Kingdom present everywhere? What do you seek today? What hopes and desires are within? Jesus gladly shares everything He has with you. Seek first His Kingdom.

"This Is Jesus, King Of The Jews." (V-37)

Thought

Their minds were too small. They were awed by earthly kings. Jesus didn't waste His time wanting to rule an earthly Kingdom. He was the Father's anointed. He understood His role from the earliest years of Nazareth. A kingdom of power and glory awaited Him and all who believed.

Application

That Kingdom is yours, too. In Jesus, you are the Father's child, heir to the power and the glory. Don't let your mind be too small. Don't be enticed by this world's kingdom when a heavenly crown awaits you.

"So you are the one who was going to destroy the temple and rebuild it in three days!" (V-40)

Thought

That misunderstood statement allows the people to write off the miracles and teachings of Jesus. Those words block all the powerful teachings. They provide an excuse, and preclude a confession of true faith. It is always easier to dismiss Jesus, than to believe in Him.

275

A dismissal ends the commitment. Believing only begins it.

Application
Don't dismiss Jesus! Don't put Him away! Don't use a slogan, a new theology, a clever half truth to keep His Kingdom at arm's length. Set aside, instead, your own words and your own plans and let the Kingdom come.

"Save yourself, why don't you? Come down off that cross if you are God's Son!" (V-40)

Thought
Saving Himself and the whole world is exactly what Jesus is doing. Because He is God's Son, He stays on the cross.

The people don't grasp this. The cross goes against all their ideas of life. They don't see the victory. They don't behold the Kingdom's doors swinging open to receive God's First-born.

Application
Jesus will save you. First, you must see clearly what you must be saved from and what you are saved for.

You are saved from selfishness, your own will, and your small world. You are saved for service to others, for God's will, and for the Kingdom.

The Chief Priests, the Scribes and the Elders also joined in the jeering. (V-41)

Thought
All had confronted Jesus and had been overcome by His teachings. So they took another course. They appealed to the Roman power they detested. Now they could jeer and deride. No more need to face the questions Jesus raised.

276

Application

How do you handle Jesus' questions? Jesus asks you, "Where are you going?" and "What do you seek?" Don't try to stifle and kill those questions. They contain the Kingdom. Don't set them aside. Answer them and receive eternal life.

CHAPTER 81
THE FINAL HOUR (27:45-56)

There was darkness over the whole land until mid-afternoon. (V-45)

Thought

Darkness was Egypt's final plague before Passover. Also the light-giving bodies of sun and moon were often seen as gods, having great power. This darkness prepares for God's power. Nowhere to look now, except the cross.

Application

One by one, your lights will go out. First you will lose your physical and mental agility; then long time friends; then your ability to work. If this world is all you have, then these losses will mean despair. If you have chosen the Kingdom, then they will merely signal that God's power and glory are coming to you.

"My God, my God, why have you forsaken me?" (V-46)

Thought

Jesus always taught trust and confidence. Even now, Jesus doesn't budge. The darkness which covered the whole land, seems to enter and pierce Him. He is abandoned, even His inner faith-light grows dim. Yet, His will doesn't waver from the Father's.

Application

Believing and choosing the Kingdom, doesn't free you from every darkness. Unending light comes only with the eternal dawning of the Kingdom. Even in darkness, don't budge in your resolve. Keep your will one with the Father's. The glory is about to be yours.

...he soaked it in cheap wine, and sticking it on a reed, tried to make him drink. (V-48)

Thought

This was a solitary, lonely act. It was totally unable to save Jesus, and was done while others would deride. However, the Kingdom had come to this soldier. He had done all he could for Jesus. The results didn't matter. That the act didn't help much, wasn't important. The glory of Jesus had begun in his heart.

Application

Let your heart be stirred this day. Everything important is really small and little. The Kingdom comes to you in tiny inspirations, quiet movings within. The Spirit touches you. He moves you to help others. Don't wait, don't hesitate. Move quickly to help.

Meanwhile the rest said, "Leave him alone. Let's see whether Elijah comes to his rescue." (V-49)

Thought

They didn't understand. The Kingdom doesn't come to those who say "Let's see if something happens." God's work had already happened in the charitable deed. They looked for the outside wonders, when really the Kingdom works within.

Application

Don't sit back and say "If I see wonders, I'll respond." God's wonders are already in your heart. Recognize

278

His gifts in your thoughts. Rejoice in your desires for the Kingdom. Great signs will happen when you respond to the Kingdom within.

Once again Jesus cried out in a loud voice, and then gave up his spirit. (V-50)

Thought
This cry was a victory shout. Jesus had persevered to the end. The Kingdom had come. The light was restored to the lampstand. Evil was banished. A strange victory! The opponent was sin, accepted mystically by Jesus into His own blood. Now the blood had been shed. Sin was cast out. The Lamb was sanctified by the sacrifice.

Application
That victory is yours by your Baptismal mystery. You are once more God's child, brought back after a period of exile. Be attracted by the cross. Remember what Jesus did for you. Cherish your victory. Seek your glory in Jesus.

Suddenly the curtain of the sanctuary was torn into two from top to bottom. (V-51)

Thought
The old wineskins can't contain the new wine. The former sanctuary with sacrifices of goats and calves, is inadequate. The Father will build a new sanctuary. He will raise up this crucified body. The prophecy is true. The old is destroyed because it can't hold the new. The new will be ready by the third day.

Application
Accept God's ways. Wait to see His plan. Don't do everything your way. Jesus gives a different wisdom, a better plan, a new covenant. All are beyond your ideas. Wait on the Lord! Then rejoice when He comes.

279

The centurion and his men who were keeping watch over Jesus were terror-stricken... (V-54)

Thought
Did these feelings lead anywhere? Did they follow through on this obvious invitation to believe? Did they approach the women and ask "could you tell me more about this Jesus?" Or, did the feelings pass quickly, becoming only a memory?

Application
How often have you seen God's wonders? Or been struck by the obvious overpowering presence of the Kingdom? What happened to you? Did you follow through? Were these moments doors that opened a new life for you? Or were they just passing moments, buried now in your memory? Well, dig them out and take the next steps into the Kingdom.

CHAPTER 82
DEATH'S AFTERMATH (27:57-66)

...a wealthy man from Arimatheus arrived, Joseph by name, he was another of Jesus' disciples. (V-57)

Thought
So many different people were touched by Jesus. He changed the poor, rich, sinners, tax collectors. All had their gift, their part to play in the Kingdom. Some left all to follow. Others served Him in exactly the same circumstances as before their conversion. All were disciples, losing their lives in the new words preached by Jesus.

280

Application

Are you His disciple? What guides your life? What word do you trust in? On what teachings do you base your life? Reflect on those questions. You only gain the Kingdom if you are His disciple.

Thereupon Pilate issued an order for its release. (V-58)

Thought

Everything fell into place. Just enough time before sunset; the tomb nearby; the willing Joseph of Arimathea; and finally, Pilate's permission.

The disciples didn't wait; didn't quarrel; didn't waver. They moved quickly, knowing God had given them this task.

Application

When God's word is your foundation, you will frequently realize that He gives you tasks. These are in keeping with our time and gifts. When this happens, move quickly into the task. Do it simply. Gather others whom God sends to help. This is how the Kingdom is built upon earth.

Joseph wrapped it in fresh linen and laid it in his own new tomb. (V-60)

Thought

Joseph brings forth his best gifts, the fresh linen and a new tomb. How blessed that shroud has become! How renowned that new tomb! God used these simple gifts, blessing untold generations in the Resurrection mystery.

Application

When Jesus asks, bring Him your finest gifts, your first fruits, your most important time, your best talents. If you bless, you will be blessed beyond measure. The Kingdom abounds with gifts, so be free with your possessions.

Then he rolled a huge stone across the entrance... (V-60)

Thought
Later the stone would become a problem to the women. On Sunday they realized they would need a man's strength to roll it back. For now, it was the final gift. Nothing was spared. The tomb was complete. The believing women begin their faith-watch, even though they didn't understand what was to happen.

Application
You experience times when the tomb is sealed. A solution seems impossible. If you are a believer, though, a strange hope will remain within, - a small light, a flickering flame, a peaceful faith. Recognize God's touch upon you and begin your faith-watch until the Father acts.

Mary Magdalene and the other Mary remained sitting there, facing the tomb. (V-61)

Thought
Each had a different call. Joseph withdrew. The women stayed. All followed the Spirit. Each was faithful to God's leading. No one could tell them what to do. No one needed to tell them. They sensed God's will within themselves and were faithful to that action.

Application
You have to read your own heart. You have to sense God's actions within you. No one else can read your heart for you. Others can teach and advise you, but you won't find the Kingdom only by listening to others.

The Spirit wants to guide you by simple, inner movements. Each has a different call. Listen for yours.

The next day, the one following the Day of Preparation, the chief priests and the Pharisees called at Pilate's residence. (V-62)

Thought
Still driven by anxiety! Even Jesus' death couldn't still their fears. Their insecurity mounts. Now the fears seem absurd. A dead man rising! And these were the non-believers!

They didn't know that security is found in following Jesus, not putting Him to death. They sought peace in the wrong way.

Application
You need peace, security and freedom from fear. Where do you find them? In power? In guns? In friends? In money? Or in the Kingdom? When you seek the Kingdom; when you choose to find God and His plan; you will be at peace. Otherwise, anxiety will drive you on and on.

Otherwise his disciples may go and steal him... (V-64)

Thought
They shouldn't worry about the disciples. They were filled with their own fears. The women weren't strong enough. So, what's the problem? Nothing real. Their imaginations are running wild. Their emotions cannot be controlled. They have no foundation. Their past is filled with lies. They have chosen poorly. The have sold their inner selves for external security.

283

Application

Only you can decide to sell yourself or be true to yourself; to seek security in lies or in truth; in the world or the Kingdom; in man or in Jesus.

You decide every day. Today you will decide. Be aware of your decisions and let the Kingdom's attraction win out

---

CHAPTER 83
A NEW LIFE FOR ALL (28:1-10)

After the Sabbath, as the first day of the week was dawning. (V-1)

Thought

They waste no time. The Sabbath rest is over. The new day dawns. Where else would they be? Their hearts are in the tomb. Now their bodies will get as close as possible. Jesus is everything for them. No room for delay or half heartedness.

Application

Where is your own heart? Where are your feelings? Your interest? What comes first? What gets your undivided attention? Where do you pour out your money and your time? What fills your calendar? Answer those questions and you will see what the Kingdom means to you.

Suddenly there was a mighty earthquake, as the angel of the Lord descended from heaven. (V-2)

Thought

Jesus said in Gethsemane that His Father could send twelve legions of angels. He also predicted that at the

284

world's end, He would come accompanied by the angels. Gethsemane was not the time for angelic power. But now, on this special Sunday, the end of the world began. It was not yet time for all the angels. Here, only one was needed. But the end had begun. The Kingdom had come.

Application

See the world as passing. It's end time is already destined. Jesus' Kingdom has dawned. What do you choose? Something doomed for destruction or the Kingdom just new and beginning? Don't be fooled. The world, as you know it, is passing away. It is already subject to earthquakes, wars and atomic bombs. Do not fear. The lasting Kingdom has come, with an angel and a new earthquake.

The guards grew paralyzed with fear of him and fell down like dead men. (V-4)

Thought

Why would anyone fear an angel? What is meant by lightning and dazzling garments? All are signs of the Kingdom. The guards are paralyzed because they are unprepared. They are like dead men. This new life is too much for their unredeemed mortality.

Application

So great is the Kingdom's gift that you must prepare. How long is enough time? Hundreds of years are too short. So, don't delay. The angel, and lightning and dazzling garments give you some small idea of the Kingdom. Seeing them, realize the preciousness of Jesus' treasure.

Then the angel spoke, addressing the women; (V-5)

Thought

A beautiful tribute, "I know you are looking for Jesus, `the crucified.'" Not just for Jesus, but "crucified!" The broken, beaten, crowned body was enough for them! They didn't come asking for signs and wonders. They came to serve Jesus. No wonder they were the first to receive God's revelation.

Application

When or how God speaks to you is out of your control. How God intervenes to save you or help you is not in your hands. Those gifts will come if you serve the Lord. If you look for the crucified Jesus, God will reveal His plan to you.

"Come and see the place where he was laid. Then go quickly and tell his disciples;..." (V-7)

Thought

Notice the two actions. First, they entered deeply into the mystery. Slowly, as they investigated the tomb, the truth came upon them. Theirs would not be a partial message or a confusing story. Secondly, they had to go. God's powerful action had to be taken forth, first to the disciples, then to all the world.

Application

You can make two mistakes. You can tell others about the Kingdom before you really grasp it yourself. You can also receive the Kingdom and then tell no one.

Accept this invitation. Come and see the place. Absorb God's power in the tomb. Then tell all the Kingdom is at hand.

Suddenly, without warning, Jesus stood before them and said "Peace!" (V-9)

Thought

To those who had been so faithful, Jesus wouldn't just send an angel. Why two appearances? The first prepared for the second. Joy had already mingled with their fear. They believed the angel's word! They were ready to experience Jesus' word. The gift was complete now. They had set out for Jesus, the crucified, and ended meeting the Risen One.

Application

Jesus Himself will come to you. Others will prepare you for His coming. Others will tell you the message. At their words, you will believe, rejoice and seek the Kingdom. But that is not all. The Kingdom is still incomplete. "Suddenly, without warning" Jesus will come.

"Go and carry the news to my brothers that they are to go to Galilee where they will see me." (V-10)

Thought

The gift is for everyone! None are excluded. Even those who ran away still have a chance to see Jesus. But they have to believe the good news. They have to go to Galilee. Just how much faith they have doesn't matter. They have to believe enough to be there when Jesus comes.

Application

The gift is for you, no matter what has happened in the past. No matter how many times you disobeyed, walked away, scoffed and sinned. Where is your Galilee? Jesus will show you. Just believe and go there.

287

CHAPTER 84
TWO RESPONSES (28:11-20)

"...guard went into the city and reported to the chief priests all that had happened. "(V-11)

Thought

Just what did they say? Certainly it was in their interest to tell the true story, that a divine intervention had prevented them from carrying out their task. Still the chief priests wouldn't yield to the Kingdom. This story gives them a final chance. The words don't come from Jesus' prophecy, nor from disciples' lips, but from their own guards. External proof, no matter how abundant, never suffices for the Kingdom. The person has to bring his own good will.

Application

Recall your own life. How many signs have you of the Kingdom? From how many lips have you heard the Kingdom's story? Your parents, priests, ministers and teachers have told you the story. The words have been multiplied. The proofs given. Now bring your own good will and believe.

"They, in turn, convened with the elders and worked out their strategy, giving the soldiers a large bribe. "(V-12)

Thought

The bribe shows they believed the soldiers. Why else give the money? They wanted the story suppressed. They wanted the good news to stop with the soldiers. They wanted a strategy to safeguard their jobs, when Jesus was offering them life in His Kingdom. Even this wasn't the end. They will have another chance to believe, as the disciples preach the good news. Jesus never gives up.

Application

You've heard the gospel many times. You have been invited to the Kingdom many times. The future probably holds even more invitations. Invitations don't get you into the Kingdom. Only your "yes" opens the door. The more you say "no," the more difficult "yes" becomes. Say "yes" now.

"His disciples came during the night and stole him while we were asleep." (V-13)

Thought

Eyewitnesses were told what to say by those who weren't even there. Those supposedly "asleep" try to witness to what happened while they were sleeping. Nothing makes sense because a simple truth won't be accepted. Jesus is all He claimed to be. Accept that and there is no need for lies.

Application

Just accept Jesus. He is everything He claims. He is your Lord, your friend, your brother. He brings you the Kingdom; gives you new life; and remains with you. Accept that truth and you will be free. You can put away everything false. You have Jesus now, and He has you.

"This is the story that circulates among the Jews to this very day." (V-15)

Thought

This story robs them of the Kingdom. They cannot hear the good news because of a false story. Doubts are sown. Another version exists. The whole resurrection supposedly never happened. The disciples carried Jesus' body out, not the Heavenly Father. People are robbed of their true heritage in Jesus.

Application

Don't let anyone rob you of the Kingdom. Don't let them place other versions in you. Don't let them say the Kingdom isn't important; or what you believe doesn't matter; or that Jesus is just one of many good people who lived. Cling fast to clear doctrine. Let no one steal the good news from your heart.

"The eleven disciples made their way to Galilee." (V-16)

Thought

This is quite a different response. The disciples make a long and difficult journey. They hadn't seen as yet. They had only heard. They had no angelic appearance and explanation. Only the words of the women. Yet each, in his heart, believes enough to come.

Application

At times, you will have to follow Jesus, even though there are few signs. Maybe just someone's word. Maybe just a certain feeling in your heart that Jesus wants you somewhere. Maybe even confusion and doubt about the whole process. It's important at these times that you make your way to "Galilee."

"At the sight of him, those who had entertained doubts fell down in homage." (V-17)

Thought

Did some remain standing or did all "entertain doubts?" Even great believers, when the full reality comes, realize they believed but little. Who, "at the sight of Him" could remain standing, as if their faith could contain the mystery? It's just the opposite. The mystery gives faith.

290

Application

As the Kingdom comes, you will realize how little you believe. You will also experience peace, realizing that the Kingdom gives faith. So use your little faith to seek Jesus. When He comes, ask for more.

"...go, therefore, and make disciples of all the nations." (V-19)

Thought

Just a few moments ago, they were full of doubts. Now, they are supposed to make everyone a disciple. They can do that now. They have seen Jesus. The gift has been given. They are eyewitnesses. They have seen the Kingdom, and will never forget its beauty.

Application

You have sought the Kingdom. Let it come. Experience the gift. See its beauty. Remember the vision on the mountain. Store up its treasures. Now you are ready to make disciples.

NOTES

292